SEVEN PILLARS
of a
BIBLICAL CHURCH

Seven Pillars
of a
Biblical Church

The Vital Truths and Essential Practices for Us
to Re-Embrace God's Design for the Church

John B. Carpenter

RESOURCE *Publications* · Eugene, Oregon

SEVEN PILLARS OF A BIBLICAL CHURCH
The Vital Truths and Essential Practices for Us to Re-embrace
God's Design for the Church

Resource Publications
An Imprint of Wipf and Stock Publishers
199 W. 8th Ave., Suite 3
Eugene, OR 97401

www.wipfandstock.com

PAPERBACK ISBN: 978-1-6667-3623-6
HARDCOVER ISBN: 978-1-6667-9428-1
EBOOK ISBN: 978-1-6667-9429-8

JANUARY 20, 2022 3:06 PM

Dedicated to the faithful members
of Covenant Reformed Baptist Church

Contents

Introduction

I STOOD ON THE TRAIN PLATFORM in Tampines, Singapore, pondering what should guide the church's preaching. A few years before, on the other side of the Pacific Ocean, at Fuller Theological Seminary, I heard a winsome defense of using a lectionary – a denomination's guide through portions of the Bible appointed to be read at specific days of the year, often according to a liturgical calendar, like advent, Christmas, epiphany, lent, Good Friday, Easter, etc. It was better, so the champion of the lectionary said, than simply leaving it up to the whims of the preacher. I wasn't convinced of his solution but I could see the problem with leaving churches' feeding on the Word dependent on the preacher's feelings. That problem became acute in Singapore where I was teaching at a Bible college run by a large church. The preaching of the church almost always beat the drum of give more, do more. I listened to members on a bus lamenting that they felt exhausted. I was reading J. I. Packer's *Knowing God* and wondering how was the church to help people to know God. The church there wasn't doing that very well because it only preached what served its interests. It occurred to me, now staring out the train windows at the high-rise concrete housing blocks of Singapore, we need to preach through the Word of God, passage by passage, saying what every passage says, not fixated on a few key scriptures that help us milk the money or work out of the people. We need to go through scripture, in what I would later come to understand as expository preaching.

Later in the nineties, I was back on the other side of the world, in the Chicago area, studying the Puritans for a Ph.D. They began to show me how their theology about salvation – usually labeled "Calvinism" – impacted their churches. There was a direct connection between the gospel they preached and how they worshiped. Into this mix, at the seminary there, I stumbled across a box, unceremoniously left in a hall-way by a visiting professor, Mark Dever. I was intrigued with what he left for the taking: a booklet and cassette tape (I believe) entitled "9 Marks of a Healthy Church." I devoured it and suggested my wife interview him for her Singapore-based magazine. She did. Later, I would consume the full-length book, use it for several series of lessons and read (probably) every book recommended at the end of each chapter. I saw in it a recovery of the Puritan idea of the church, of the living connection between Puritan theology and practice. After almost twenty years of pastoring, I've digested and absorbed much of it. If in the course of this book, I sometimes, echo Dever's book without proper credit, I don't mean to plagiarize. It's just that much of it has become part of me and now comes out with me, sifted through my own experience and now, as another student of Puritanism – mostly of the New England variety –supplemented, reinterpreted, and consolidated.

I saw in the Puritans a different model of the church and ministry than I had grown up in. In Puritanism the pastor was akin to a prophet, with scripture his source of revelation. Just as Isaiah or Jeremiah would stand before the people of God and say "thus says the Lord," based on the revelation they had, the Puritan pastor was to stand before his people, with revelation from the Bible, and say "Thus says the Lord." They sang psalms, prayed and preached the Word, looked for signs of conversion, of desiring God, thanked God for every gift of providence at Thanksgiving and grieved for their sins, listening to Jeremiads, on fasting days. The Puritans understood the gospel so well that when Cotton Mather counselled a condemned murderer while escorting him to the gallows, he led the man into first an awareness of sin and then hope in Christ for satisfaction of God's wrath against that sin. The Puritans taught me how to be a pastor. I can't blame them for my failures to live up to their ideals.

Finally, my own experience in the church – and churches of various traditions – in three continents has forged these principles. We planted our church in 2008, which means, unencumbered by the traditions of a pre-established church, we were able to implement these principles, and learn some lessons from experience, sometimes painfully.

First of all, though, this is the product of Bible study. It is seven expositions of key passages of scripture, with reference to many others. It's not just theological speculation or the recovery of a tradition, as rich as our (often neglected) tradition is. The Puritans wanted to return to a Biblically pure church. So do I. Both the Puritans and I have gone back to the Bible. The result is seven pillars.

Pillars hold buildings up. The church is God's building and it needs pillars to hold it up. These seven may not be exhaustive but they are indispensable.

PILLAR 1

The Whole Counsel of God

Acts 20:17–35

EVER THOUGHT YOU UNDERSTOOD something pretty well only to be made to realize you were only seeing one side of the story? Ever start to answer a question before it was fully asked and be embarrassed that you assumed the question wrongly? Ever hear someone make a case for themselves — how wronged they were, how right they are — only to hear the other side and realize you were fooled?

I once assumed I knew something, based on an incomplete picture. I was walking down a side walk in Singapore, with a high wall on my right side. When I got to the driveway into a large parking lot, I was shocked to see, inside the half of the walled-off lot, to my right, two men arguing violently. They were speaking Mandarin so I couldn't understand them but I could tell they were very mad at each other; they were about to get into a fight. I knew if they did, I would have to break it up. I stopped in my tracks, with the wall still blocking my view of the other half of the lot. I stared at the two men arguing in one part of the parking lot. Then suddenly, just as I feared, one man took a big swing at the other man and he went flying back, like he had been hit hard. The fight had started! I had to do my duty and break up the fight. It was weird;

1

from my angle, the man who took the swing missed his target by a mile. Yet, the other guy jerked backwards like he had been hit. But . . . whatever! I could see the fight had begun. I began to walk quickly toward the two fighting men. As I reached the end of the driveway, I could see what I couldn't see before. In the half of the parking lot was a TV camera and camera man, a man with a boom mic, a lighting man, and a few other people watching the two actors! Everything I saw before was true, but I couldn't interpret it correctly until I saw the whole picture.

The worst that would have happened if I had tried to break up the two actors, would be my own embarrassment. But sometimes acting on partial perceptions can have much more dire consequences. In 2001, my family and I were living in Singapore. My son's speech therapist won a free vacation to New York City in September of 2001. Think about that: in New York City, September, 2001! On the morning of Tuesday, September 11th, 2001, as part of her prize, she was supposed to take a tour up to the top of the World Trade Center. While walking toward it she looked up and saw an airplane disappear into the side of one of the towers. From her point of view, all that she could see was the plane going into the building. Those pictures you've seen on TV over and over again show the plane hitting on one side and the explosion coming out the other side. She was looking at the side the plane hit. Her first thought was that this was some kind of movie stunt or magic trick, like David Copperfield making an illusion of a plane disappearing into a building. She said she saw so many other strange things in New York, she figured this was just another one of them. She turned to her husband and said, "Oh, what a neat effect." They kept walking straight toward the World Trade Center. Only when crowds of people began running the other way did she realize that something horrible had just happened. You can see something very important, even be an eye-witness to the worst terrorist attack, but get the exact wrong lesson and respond in exactly the wrong way, unless you get the whole picture.

That's exactly what is wrong with a lot of preaching these days. There are many preachers who aren't preaching anything that is directly false. They are just preaching one side of the story. We can rail against the false doctrines of the cults, criticize some people for their overt doctrine. But in my experience, there are far more people today who are only teaching half the story. What they declare maybe entirely true. But it isn't the entire truth. As J. I. Packer said, a half-truth presented as a whole truth is a complete untruth. Because they aren't declaring the entire truth, people can respond in exactly the wrong way. There are people who are, right now, heading toward disaster based on their true but merely partial perception.

How are we not to be among them? The Apostle Paul gives us the key in this farewell address to the elders in Ephesus in Acts 20 — "if only I may testify to the gospel," he says — and explains what the churches he's leaving behind need, what he calls "the whole counsel of God."

What Is the Whole Counsel of God?

The term is self-explanatory. First, "whole" means all, the entirety. The "counsel" means the truths God has revealed. Psalm 119:24 says, "Your testimonies are indeed my delight; they are my counselors." They are the counsel he has given us in his Word, which is "of God." In Acts 20:32, he commends the church to God and "the Word of his grace." Scripture. That would mean that things not revealed in his Word, that are "of man," just speculations about theology, debates about the end-times, politics, pop-psychology, fluff about self-esteem, a lot of the stuff that gets so much attention these days, can be skipped because much of that is not profitable. But not anything that God revealed in the Bible. We proclaim everything and it is all profitable because that message of the gospel is in all of it, including the Old Testament. The gospel of the grace of God is the scarlet thread running through the Old Testament.

Notice how important Paul deems declaring the whole message of scripture. In Acts 20:20 Paul reminds them that he "did not shrink from declaring to you anything that was profitable." He doesn't say he eventually got around to it all. He says he did not shrink; that is, he never held back, never afraid that if he teaches an unpopular doctrine they'll reject him. He never flinched from declaring everything God has said. He didn't shrink from declaring (not whispering) anything. It's not as though some things — the popular things — he said loudly and others — the unpopular — he whispered. He declared everything.

In Paul's farewell message to the church of Ephesus, in Acts 20:20, he says he's innocent of their blood because he did not hold back. He is drawing on an image from Ezekiel — the watchman (Eze. 33) — held accountable for warning. If the watchman on the wall sees danger coming, an invading army, and doesn't warn — he's afraid it will be an unpopular message — he will be held responsible. But if he warns and the people don't listen — they don't close the gate and prepare to defend themselves — then it's not his fault when the city is destroyed. He did what he was supposed to do: warn. He might not win the people; he must warn. The church is not held accountable for winning. We might not win. We must warn. There are times when faithfulness will bring loss and suffering, as it did for Paul as he left the Ephesians and went — knowingly — into prison. As he went, he warned them.

Those committed to teaching the whole counsel of God may sometimes lose people who can't accept certain teachings. Those who hate the idea that their salvation is totally outside their control, that God is sovereign, will want to go where they can be inspired by pep talks that tell them that they can do whatever they set their mind to, that they are David in the Goliath story. Others are repelled by the idea that Jesus teaches church discipline (Mt. 18:15–18); the "Jesus" they believe in makes people comfortable in their sin. Some are so attached to their favorite end-times theories — including ones that aren't really taught in scripture — that they will drift off elsewhere when consistent, expository preaching means they don't get to hear them. Others can't stand to have their autonomy (self-rule), their individualism, and their consumer attitude called into question. They assume everything exists for their consumption — marriage, family, even the Bible, salvation, worship, the church, the Lord himself. When it finally gets through to them that they really are supposed to care for a Body to which they are to be covenanted, that the church isn't like a restaurant, geared to serving them, they'll decide that they deserve a break from that church. Those who've been raised on the milk of the consumer-driven philosophy that the faith, Jesus, the Father, the Holy Spirit, certainly the church all exist to give me "my best life now," will decide, if that basic attitude is challenged, "I'll go try another one."

The consumeristic individualism that the culture has inculcated in modern people, will make them react when it finally dawns on them that we're saying that we're supposed to transform that basic self-centered attitude for the Lord and his Body. They find that repulsive. We want to win them. We'll try our best to present everything as winsomely as we can. But sometimes faithfulness means warning without winning. I don't mean to make excuses for not reaching people, for staying small. We should be eager to grow. A healthy church wants to grow. But if we have to make a choice between warning or winning, we had better choose warning. If we hold back any part of the message and people continue to head toward disaster because they can't see the whole picture, we will be judged, we will have, in some way, their blood on our hands. To be free of the guilt of the souls of others, we need (as a Body, together) to be showing people the whole picture.

How Do We Get the Whole Counsel of God?

First, we need to recognize that we all have biases. Some of the most dangerous people are those who don't know they are biased, especially if they become professors or editors! We like certain ideas and we dislike others. We have blind spots. We see certain things (whether it's there or not) and we totally miss other things that are there. When we come to the Bible, we naturally gravitate toward those themes and books that we prefer and think we understand. It's like ruts in a dirt road. We keep following the ruts, no matter where it leads. It's easier than forging a new path.

Therefore, we need a disciplined regimen of going through all of scripture. That's why you, in your private Bible reading need to try to read the entire Bible over a year or two, not just camp on a few favorite passages or let devotionals spoon feed you a verse here and there. For a church together, we should intentionally shift around to all parts of the Bible, in the Old Testament the Law, Prophets and Writings and in the New Testament the gospels (including Acts) and the letters (including Revelation.) The preaching normally should be series consisting of weeks or months, passage by passage through whole portions of larger books, like the first eleven chapters of Genesis or the passion narratives in the gospels, and go through whole books, like Romans.

We believe, what Paul wrote later to Timothy, "all scripture is inspired by God" and all of it is profitable; all of it is useful; we need all of it. This means normally covering more of the Bible than just a verse or two every sermon. Some preachers seem to treat it as a badge of honor how slowly they are crawling through the Bible. But if it takes years to get through Romans, the church will likely be unable to hear the whole counsel of God. A respected, notable preacher took twelve years to preach through Romans. That means that a child who becomes old enough to understand what's going on in church, about age 6, will have grown up in the church, then perhaps go away to college having never heard preaching anything else, missing much of the Bible. Preach the Bible as it is inspired, in passages, not to impress people with how much content can be squeezed out of a single phrase.

Be careful of any teaching or teacher who tells you that some parts of the Bible aren't for us any more, that they belong to another era, that we can "unhitch" it from our faith today. To get the whole counsel of God, you need the whole Word of God, including the Old Testament. So, for example, our church methodically read, and sing and pray through all the Psalms. We read, sing (a paraphrased version set to the tune of a well-known hymn) and pray a psalm for every service, one-by-one through the whole book of Psalms. That exposes us to things to sing and pray about we would not think of on our own. Every year we try to preach from at least a portion of the Law, Prophets, Writings, gospels and epistles.

How are we to see the whole picture? The Apostle Paul tells us, one way, in Colossians 3:16, is to sing. Let the Word of Christ dwell in you richly by singing: singing Psalms, hymns, and spiritual songs. Our own songs will reflect our tastes, our culture. So we need to sing psalms too, all of them, knowing that when we do that, we'll soon find ourselves singing and praying things that seem incredibly bizarre to our modern ears. It's like someone who's only been given vegetables to eat, suddenly given some meat. At first it will feel strange in your mouth, even hard to swallow. But keep chewing on it and eventually you'll begin to like it!

Some will say, "You don't need to be so regimented. Follow the lead of the Spirit." I heard of a man who dropped out of church when he learned the pastor prepares his messages ahead of time. But what better leading of the Spirit can there than what the Holy Spirit actually wrote and inspired? In other words, we teach and preach the Word of God as it is given to us. We don't come up with the topics we want to hear about and then selectively take the scriptures we think support our beliefs about those topics. That is exactly the advice given today on how to attract people to church: preach the topics people want to hear. If we do that, when will we ever get to telling them about their need for salvation, about sin and judgment and damnation? How will they ever understand why it was necessary for Jesus to die on the cross, to buy their salvation with his blood?

Do we really believe that God knew what he was doing when he inspired the books in the Bible as they are? Or do we deep down wish the Bible was in topics that we're interested in: six ways to find a spouse, seven steps to a happy marriage, eight signs of the end times, nine keys to prosperity! True arrogance is editing the Bible to be the way we want it to be. It is saying that if God really knew what he was doing, this is how he should have put the Bible together. True humility bows before the Word and admits that God was right all along. Paul points to his humility at the beginning in Acts 20:19. He says he served "the Lord with all humility." That's precisely why he taught them "the whole counsel of God": because he was too humble to imagine he knew better than the Lord about what to teach the people. The way the Holy Spirit led scripture is better than our opinions about what parts of scripture to select.

To see the whole picture, we need to talk about it. In Acts 20:20 Paul says he went from house to house, visiting people, talking about the Bible. He didn't talk just about football, the weather, politics, health but the whole counsel of God. Christians should want to talk to each other about what the Word teaches. That's why in our church our Wednesday evening meeting consists in talking about the passage for Sunday's coming sermon. We're not trying to answer all our questions in that first reading; we're certainly not taking an "everyone's view is equally true" approach. We're trying to pique our interest and focus our minds about that passage. Then we can gather and hear the sermon on Sunday morning with a mind and heart already geared to what the passage is about. That we're willing to listen to other Christians, means they will bring to our attention passages we might not know about, something we overlooked because we were dwelling on our favorite few verses. To see the whole picture, we need the whole Body. *Sola scriptura* — scripture alone is our final authority — doesn't mean solo scriptura (just me and scripture).

How are we to see the whole picture? We still need preaching. When Paul said "teaching you in public" he means preaching to gatherings. One of the keys to hearing the whole counsel of God is expository preaching; that is exposing — explaining and declaring — what the passage says. As Mark Dever says, in expository preaching, the main point of a passage of scripture is the main point of the message. Normally that is what we do: look at whole passages, seeking to see the whole picture. We can feed on everything God has provided for us. Like someone eating a well-balanced diet, we can grow up healthy and strong. But that means that you need to eat it, to listen; to come prepared to listen; pray ahead of time for a good appetite, for eagerness to listen; take notes if that helps you listen; listen again on-line if you need more. Paul preached publicly. That means you need to gather publicly, with the church.

To see the whole picture, we not only study it, we experience it. We have to do it, to feel it, to practice it. Our actions also teach. We can deny, or obscure, part of the counsel of God by not living it. If we say, "it's more blessed to give than to receive" but we simply splurge on ourselves, people will see it's just empty words. If we say, "We want to be a biblical church" and then don't sing psalms — even when the Bible says to do it — or don't practice church discipline — because we live in a culture that hates discipline — we teach with our lives that those passages can be ignored. If we say Jesus is for all kinds of people but our churches are only made of our kind of people, people notice what they see, not what we say. If we say, "I love the Lord," we quote Psalm 45, "My heart overflows with a pleasing theme; I address my verses to the king," but then worship, singing to the Lord is dreary or routine or boring, there's no sense of being pleased by worshipping the Lord, then our lives declare that Psalm 45 isn't true, at least not for us. If we say, "I love the Word of God," but then we skip on Bible study, we can't muster the self-discipline to endure it when it's not always exciting and immediately inspiring, our lives teach something else. If we say, "I want to serve the Lord," but then we don't feel, like the Apostle Paul in Acts 20:24, we account our cozy life-style as more valuable than the low pay of a ministry or our neat minivan as more important than transporting rambunctious kids to hear the gospel of the grace of God, then our actions teach we prefer our comfort.

Notice how Paul shows his vibrant experience with God in Acts 20. He begins by pointing to "how I lived," in 20:17. Twice, in 20:19 and 31, he mentions his tears. Paul was a passionate man. He deeply felt the value of what he taught. He experienced God himself, especially God the Holy Spirit, in what he was teaching. Notice that in 20:22 he speaks of being "constrained" or "bound" by the Spirit. Then in the next verse he speaks of how the Holy Spirit has been testifying to him of what is going to happen. These were not just theories about abstract doctrines. He was talking about realities he was experiencing. He was a doer of the Word. He lived it.

Unlike some people today who want "experiences" with the Spirit just for the thrill of it, as a drug to escape from the trials of this life, Paul's experience with the Spirit actually led him into more trials in this life. Why does he follow the Spirit into chains and suffering? Acts 20:24 could be Paul's personal mission statement: "But I do not account my life of any value nor as precious to myself, if only I may finish my course and the ministry that I received from the Lord Jesus, to testify to the gospel of the grace of God." Paul had, what the prophet Jeremiah described as "fire in his bones" (Jer. 20:9). This was his life. It should be the life of our church. We're not so concerned with being respectable or being big or successful or being on the cutting edge or being comfortable in our old-time religion. If only we may finish the course laid out for us, the ministry of testifying to the gospel of the grace of God! Not just to talk about it but to practice it. To run that course.

Why Do We Need the Whole Counsel of God?

Why would we want to give up all the advantages of cutting and pasting the parts of the Bible we like, and using it for ourselves, ignoring the rest? After all, why not give the customer what he wants? "The customer is king." People want to hear about how to be successful, how to find the right spouse, how to raise nice kids. They don't want to hear about their sin; certainly not about God's judgment on sin; certainly not that their sins are so bad that their only hope is if the perfect man, God himself, took those sins on himself on the cross, that they needed to be bought from death, that it took blood to purchase them. There are many teachings of the Bible that are not very popular. So, why bother? Give them the parts they like, and just sweep the rest under a rug, call some Bible teachings "a family secret." The third and last question is "why is the whole counsel of God necessary?"

Without everything God has revealed, the message we present falls apart. If we only speak about grace and never sin, judgment and repentance, people think they are saved no matter how they live. They continue in sin. They don't know what they are supposed to be saved from: the wrath of God, the penalty, power and eventually the presence of sin. If we only present what people must do — be good, don't commit adultery, or steal, or lie, go to church (at least occasionally) — then people become proud of their life and religion and don't think they need the grace of God. Why is the whole picture necessary? Because without it, we become badly nourished, like someone who only eats sweets. Only hearing the "sweet" themes we naturally prefer is like only eating sweet foods we crave. If we only drink Coke and eat cake and ice-cream, eventually we will get fat and sick. A poor diet makes you vulnerable. So too does a poor spiritual diet. Paul, in Acts 20:29 to 31, mentions the "savage wolves" that will attack. The savage wolves are looking for weak strays, those who don't hear the whole counsel of God. When we miss some of what God has revealed, we will be vulnerable to wolves. Wolves are prowling around — on TV, on the internet, sometimes knocking at your door — looking for our weak spots, looking for people who only know part of the truth, half-truths that become complete untruths. So, in Acts 20:32, Paul commends us to "the word of his grace," scripture, not tradition or a magisterium (a hierarchy of church leaders supposedly tracing their origins to the apostles.) In his absence the apostle entrusts the church to God's Word which comes from and shows us God's grace.

Paul was a passionate man; he shed tears in his zeal for God's truth and his care for the church. In Acts 20:17–35, he calls us to have the same care. Notice how he refers to the Church. In Acts 20:28 and 29 he twice calls the church "the flock." In 20:28, it is the "Church of God," the people whom God has called for himself. The Church should be precious to us because it is precious to God. So precious, he bought it. God purchased it with what was precious to Him: his own blood: "the Church of God which he obtained — or bought — with his own blood." Quite a striking statement of Jesus' divinity. It is God's blood which bought the Church because Jesus is God. Jesus cared for the church so much, he was willing to bleed for it; to die for it.

Why do we believe and teach the Whole Word of God? Because it protects the Church, this precious gathering of people that God especially purchased. Jesus said, "It is more blessed to give than to receive" and he gave his life. He practiced what he taught. He gave his blood because he loves the church, the flock, the diaspora of God's people spread to the ends of the earth. The Word of God in the flesh commends us to the Word of God in scripture, to keep us, to nourish us, to defend us, a pillar to hold us up, to give us our inheritance: the salvation he spent his blood to buy. I commend it to you too.

PILLAR 2

God According to God

Exodus 34:5-7

HAVE YOU EVER WANTED something to be true so badly, you fooled yourself into believing it must be true? I so wanted the corona virus to go away after a fifteen-day lockdown, I was surprised when it was extended another month and then indefinitely. Some people so want to have a job in something where there are no jobs, they'll get in student loan debt studying philosophy or gender studies. American Idol always started out with people who so believe they can sing, who embarrass themselves trying and get mad at the guy who tells them they can't. Some people so believe their children are little darlings they don't discipline them. If someone else tries, they'll think there's something wrong with those people. People are so attached to the way they want things to be, they will believe that's the way they are. Perhaps, they are "in love." Everyone else can tell this isn't going to work out; the other person isn't good for them, or just plain isn't good. But they so want it to be right, they see their loved one with rose colored glasses; they will deny the obvious, and won't come to terms that this is wrong until maybe the spouse walks out. Or, if we're talking about a woman, she won't admit he's no good until he beats her badly. Maybe not even then.

Today people believe that if they want something to be true, then it must be true. If they believe that they are female but the biology says they are male, what they want — not what is — is the reality. Modern culture now insists that we enable that; go along with it. Some Western countries are making it illegal to call someone who wants to be the sex they aren't, by the sex they are. There's even a term for it now: "misgendering." We think our desires, our self-identification, can over-ride reality.

Some women so want children that they will convince themselves that they are pregnant when they're not. There is a condition known as false pregnancy, clinically termed "pseudocyesis": the belief that you are expecting a baby when you are not really carrying a child. Women with pseudocyesis have many, if not all, the symptoms of pregnancy, even the distended abdomen with the exception of an actual baby. They so want a child that their mind fools their body that they have one until it comes time to deliver and there's nothing to deliver.

People believe that if they want something to be true, then it must be true. But eventually reality will come crashing down. Simon Cowell will tell us bluntly that we're atrocious (with a British accent). Or your darling child needs to be bailed out of jail, divorce papers are served, or when you have to go the emergency room for being beaten. Or when you're not able to deliver a baby because there isn't one.

So, how do you like to think of God? Do you shape God to be the person you want him to be?

Reality can be very painful but it's also very stubborn. It will catch up to us, sooner or later. With God, we could go our entire lives fantasizing that he is as we want him to be. Unlike with those other things, we won't get a no-show baby or some other piece of tangible evidence to tell us otherwise. At least not yet. Right now, we have the Bible. We have his description of what he said he is like. The question is whether we are willing to put aside the fantasy god we so much want to believe in and embrace the true One who has revealed himself in his Word.

How Do You Like to Think About God?

A few years ago, a major denomination put on commercials a voice, claiming to be God, sentimentally appealing for people to return to Him. Saying things like, "Please come back to Me, I've been waiting so long." God sounds so desperate, lonely and needy. You'd have to be heartless not to have pity on that poor ol' god begging you for just a little time. Starting several years ago, bill-boards began to appear with quotes, saying they were from God. They were put up by a group called "God Speaks," except God didn't speak, at least not any of those things. They were made up by advertising people. I saw a few of them on a trip once. Cute stuff, like, "All I know is, . . . everything. — God." "Let's meet at my house before the game. — God." "I love you, I love you, I love you. — God." While none of it was directly unbiblical, I wonder, why anyone would think they can make up quotes from God? If you really want quotes from God, you could go to where he has spoken. Where do quotes like that come from? I guess, from how they like to think about God.

How do you like to think about God? A pillar of a biblical church is that it teaches about God what he has revealed about himself, not just what popular opinion says, or it gets the results they want or is their tradition. In a Biblical church, the God who is worshipped is the true God who has spoken for himself.

In Exodus 34:5–7 God reveals himself. Here we have God describing God. This isn't an opinion among many opinions; something someone "shared" a while ago, to be placed alongside whatever you or I want to "share" about what we happen to feel God is like, while we celebrate the diversity of each other's opinions. Here we see what the Lord likes to think about himself. This is the rock-solid, absolute truth.

First, let's look at the context of Exodus 34:5–7. God's weightiness, his glory and power, has been seen vividly in the deliverance of his people from what was one of the great super-powers of that time. The Lord calls Moses at the burning bush, sends him to Pharaoh, unleashes the 10 plagues — or blows — on Egypt, and finally drowns Pharaoh's army in the sea. Then God's holiness is illustrated by the laws, starting with the 10 commandments in Exodus 20, then all the other laws with their punishments against sin. The sacrificial system portrays the wages of sin. With every animal hauled up to the altar and killed, they were to see that is the cost of sin. The tabernacle architecturally portrays God's holiness. He is set apart in a restricted area called the "holy of holies."

Then, while all of this is being revealed to Moses on Mount Sinai, the people of Israel decide to make an idol. In Exodus 32 is the famous story of the Golden Calf. Aaron declares a feast to not some made-up god, but to the Lord. This was his opinion of who God was. This was how he liked to think about God. When Moses sees that — how his brother Aaron likes to think about God — he breaks the tablets of the ten commandments, destroys the idol, pounds it to dust, puts the dust in a stream, and makes the people drink it; then he calls some faithful men from the tribe of Levi and dispatches them to kill the worst of the idolaters in Israel, executing about 3,000 men. Then, Moses intercedes for Israel. As part of his intercession, in 33:18, Moses asks, "Please show me your glory." Then the Lord says he will; he will pass before Moses, but to spare his life, the Lord will hide him in a cleft of the rock. Then comes this passage.

The Lord describes himself. He has not left us to our own guesses as to who he might be; what he might be like. In the words of the title to a famous Francis Schaeffer book he is, "The God Who is There and he is not silent."

God's Name

Then, the Lord descends in a cloud — to portray God's glory — and proclaims his own name: "The LORD, the LORD." God's special revelation of himself, Yahweh. This was the Name given at the burning bush: Yahweh, "I am who I am." Here, now, simply, "I AM." We see in this name at least three vital truths about God: he is transcendent, eternal, and absolute.

First, transcendent means that God is over and above us in a way that can never be overcome by us. We can't bridge the gap and become God. Some of the cults teach that God is of the same species that we are, just more evolved. Lorenzo Snow, fifth president of the Latter Day Saints Church (the Mormons), stated that "As man now is, God once was; as God now is, man may become." That's how Mormons like to think about God. But it's not how the Lord has revealed himself. He is the "I Am" in that he is the One who eternally is, who is self-existent, derived and dependent on no one else. We name ourselves by where we come from, our family name is passed down to us. I'm derived from the Carpenter family. In their culture, one was named after their father. So Moses was "Moses son of Amram." I would be, John son of Walter. Our names showing who we are derived from. But the Lord reveals himself as the one who is named after no one else, derived from no one else. He is the I Am.

As the "I AM," he is eternal. He is not the "I was" or the "I will be," as though he is under time, subject to time, aging and changing, subject to forces outside of him shaping him. There was never a time when he was not and there never will be a time when he is no longer.

Because he is the I Am — underived, eternal — he is the absolute, the standard. His opinions are the truth. If he said it, it is true just because he said it. It's impossible for God to lie because when he says something he makes it true. He spoke, "Let there be light" and there was light. He spoke the worlds into existence. He doesn't just have a view of things in competition with other persons' view of things. His view is the way things are. He is the I am. If the way you like to think about God is different than what God declares, you're wrong.

God's Goodness

God here says he is merciful and gracious, slow to anger, and abounding in steadfast love: God has mercy, grace, patience, and loyalty to his people. Really all these are several different ways of describing God's overflowing love, his exuberant goodness; like looking at several facets of a beautiful diamond, gazing at how its sides sparkle. Let's take them in order: mercy, grace, slowness to anger. God's mercy is his goodness toward those in distress. Two blind men once cried out to Jesus (in Mt. 9:27). They were in great distress. So they pleaded, "Have mercy on us." Mercy is not receiving what we deserve. We deserve punishment. We deserve blindness or whatever effects of the Fall come our way.

This is why the Puritans developed the holiday of Thanksgiving. They striped away all the traditional church holidays, including Christmas and Easter but gave us Thanksgiving. Thanksgiving days were the flip side of Fasting Days. John Cotton (1585–1652) wrote, "Besides the celebration of the Lord's Day every week, we sometimes upon extraordinary occasions, either of notable judgements, do set apart a day of humiliation, or upon special mercies we set apart a day of thanksgiving." When you see, first, that God perfectly rules all our affairs — the doctrine of providence — then, that we as sinners deserve no good thing and, yet, God has seen fit to give us life, food, clothing, family, friends, and all kinds of good, then it's not because we deserve them but because God has been merciful. The conclusion is thanksgiving.

Then there is God's amazing grace. If mercy is not getting what we deserve, grace is getting what we don't deserve. It is receiving goodness when we only deserve punishment. The apostle Paul, writing in Romans 3:23–24, says, "All have sinned and fall short of the glory of God." We all deserve punishment. But there is more because God is gracious. "And are justified freely by his grace through the redemption that came by Christ Jesus." He has made a way for us to be right with God, despite our sin. That is an act of grace.

Then there is God's patience. He is slow to anger, even though he is perfect in his standards. God's patience is his goodness toward those who continue to sin over a period of time. He's not a hot head. He doesn't lose his temper at a little irritation. His anger doesn't flare up suddenly.

In 2003 my family and I got to travel the whole country, from shore to shore. We camped most of the time. Of course, when you camp, you've got to have a camp fire. I noticed a big difference between the wood in the west and the east. In the west, like Montana, we could start a camp fire immediately. The wood ignited quickly and burned brightly. It was also burnt up quickly. But in the east, once in a camp ground in Maryland just outside Washington, DC, the wood took so long to get lit I gave up on it, thinking the fire had gone out. After about an hour, the wood started to catch fire. Once it was on fire, it will burn long and hot. God here says, he is not like that dry tinder out west, easily ignited. But don't think he can't burn long and hot.

Then, we see here, God's covenant love, his steadfast love. There is a special Old Testament word, *hesed*, that appears twice in Exodus 34:5-7. God is "abounding in *hesed*." It is best translated as "steadfast love." It's often paired, like here, with "faithfulness." *Hesed* already implies faithfulness. Pairing it with faithfulness accentuates that. True love is unwavering; it bears all things, believes all things, hopes all things, endures all things. It doesn't fail. It doesn't go away because it gets bored with you; because it finds something better up the road. It's committed, relational love. The New English Bible translates it as "ever constant and true." It appears again near the beginning of verse 7. It is God's covenant love: his loyal commitment to be good to his people. God's love expresses itself in covenanting.

Some modern people decry the practice of church covenants as cultic. Church covenants are actually derived from the Puritans who understood that the church is a body of believers knit together, comprising a regenerate membership. To join a church was to commit to be in a covenant with the other members. Samuel Danforth (1666–1727) led, in Taunton, Massachusetts, societies for prayer, encouraging family worship, and self-disciplining of youth. A revival ensued in 1705, which was celebrated, in Puritan style, by a covenant renewal service. Such covenants were formal commitments, based on scripture, calling on the members to pledge to specific behavior, like "to watch over one another with an affectionate care," and "to contribute cheerfully and regularly to the support of the ministry, the expenses of the church." A standard one was passed down to Baptist churches, some still hanging on their walls as curiosities of a by-gone age. The common objection today is that asking Christians to subscribe to such a covenant is excessively controlling. But God himself covenants. If we're to be like Him, how can we object to covenanting?

God emphasizes the constancy, the firmness of this committed love by declaring that he also abounds in faithfulness. Faithfulness is already inherent in "*hesed*" but he wants to make sure we understand that he endures. He emphasizes the perseverance of God's commitment to his people, which is why we believe in the preservation of the saints; that all those God has chosen to love, he will preserve to the end. He will hold us fast, because of steadfast love and faithfulness.

The way many people like to think of someone being "good" is that he (or she) is good for helping them get what they want. You can tell them about all kinds of bad things so-and-so did and they'll reply, "But he never did me wrong." Germans in the 1930s thought, "Hitler isn't hurting me." So, for such people, God is "good" if he enables them to get healthy, wealthy, inspires them to do their best, comforts them when they're feeling down. To them God is "good" in that he is a tool under their control to achieve their goals. How do you like to think about God? Probably as good, but is it a goodness for you?

God's Holiness

Once, at a mega church, I saw a video full of quotes from the Bible about God, which even quoted from Exodus 34:5–6 but then, suddenly stopped right after "forgiving iniquity, transgression, and sin; in the middle of verse 7, it cut away, just before the "but" and then went on to quote other sweet passages about the Lord, selectively editing the Bible to serve their purpose. But, the "but" is there.

Today, many want only to think of God as their Father who will love and accept them no matter what they do; a celestial cheer-leader or teddy bear or inspirer; that they can get to him any way they choose, that broad is the road that leads to life, and everyone can get there if they're sincere. It's moralistic, therapeutic deism: God is pleased by our morality, our niceness; he exists to soothe our feelings, to comfort us, like Linus' blanket; He's not in direct control of all things. He's emotionally close but effectively far away, not a sovereign God of providence ruling all things, judging sin.

The moralistic, therapeutic deistic god is pictured for us in the popular "Footprints" poem. It presents a god we don't need most of the time, only during the "very lowest and saddest times," times that are apparently out of his control. That's how many people today like to think about God. But then comes the "but" in God's self-description in Exodus 34:5–7. It shows us also that God is holy and just. He's like Aslan in "The Lion, the Witch and the Wardrobe." A child asks, "Is Aslan a tame lion." The answer? No, he's not tame. But he's good.

Coming directly from the mouth of God himself — God according to God — God tells us that he has wrath (anger) toward sin. Exodus 34:5–7 tells us that God thinks of himself as intensely hating sin, burning long and hot against it. This is not just an Old Testament theme, as though God cooled down after the Old Testament and mellowed out for the New Testament. No. Even in the famous third chapter of John — the "God so loved the world" chapter — it says, "whoever does not obey the Son shall not see life, but the wrath of God remains on him" (John 3:36).

God says he is merciful, gracious, loyally committed to his people. But then there's "who will by no means clear the guilty, visiting the iniquity of the fathers on the children." It is a strange "but," isn't it? He goes, in the space of one sentence, to saying he will forgive iniquity, transgression, and sin to, to "who will by no means clear the guilty." "By no means." You aren't going to be able to sweet talk your way past the judgment seat. There is no possible way that our sins will not be fully paid for. Our sins aren't going to just be swept under the rug. Forgiveness does not mean he says,

"Aw shucks, you're so cute, how can I hold it against you." He will "by no means" clear the guilty. The scary part: we're all guilty.

So, how does God forgive sin without clearing the guilty? How are both of these truths possible? If we are all guilty and if God will not clear the guilty then aren't we all doomed? How can he be both merciful and still visit every sin?

The Lord visited our iniquities on Jesus himself. The Apostles tell us, in Acts 4:27, that God used Herod and Pontius Pilate to kill Jesus. God didn't just sit back and let it happen. The Father was not just a victim. God himself acted. He made sure that Jesus would die on a cross. Herod and Pilate did what God predestined that they would do. Isaiah 53:10 says, "It was the will of the LORD to crush Him." The one human being throughout all history who deserved no punishment suffered the most horrible punishment so God wouldn't have to visit our iniquities on us. He visited them on the Son. God took our guilt and put it on him so that now, we're not guilty. So he can both visit our sin with the judgment it deserves and let us go unpunished.

He did that because God is, on the one hand, merciful, loyally committed to loving his people, and, on the other, not willing to let the guilty go unpunished. So he accounted Jesus to be sin for us and punished him for us. He did that so he could be merciful to us. Without that sacrifice there remains, as it says in John 3:36, no option except that the "wrath of God abides" on us. He visits iniquity.

Notice the way that is put, at the end of Exodus 34:7, "visiting the iniquity." It's an active verb. He is getting up, into action, and intervenes to aggressively punish sin. He "visits" the iniquity of the fathers on the children. Some want to merely say it's like the sins of drunkenness or abuse being passed down in families, from one generation to another. God lets it happen. That's true. But this passage goes a big step beyond that. It's not just laws of nature outside of his control. Notice that it doesn't just say he lets generations bear the consequences for their actions. (That is a biblical truth, but he says more than that here.) It says he does it. He takes the initiative. God intervenes and judges and punishes sin. Is that how we've been thinking about God?

Reckless Love?

How we think of God has a direct impact on how we live together in the church, how we worship and relate to each other. If we think God has a "reckless love" instead of a "steadfast" love, we're probably not very constant, not steady, not faithful like Him. We think love is a gushy feeling instead of a commitment. We think breaking commitments is no big deal, no real sin. Commitments are just words people say and we don't actually take them seriously; after all, we serve a god of "reckless love," who's all about feeling good for us, puffing our self-esteem, a divine teddy bear. If we mistrustingly complain that His sovereign plan for our life didn't follow our expectations, he whispers, in response, "My precious child, I love you."

If we stop in the middle of Exodus 34:7, like that mega church video, we might think we are supposed to casually excuse sin like nothing happened; that we wink at it, or maybe occasionally we can grimace at it, if it's really bad. If we do not think we are supposed to effectively deal with sin, to confront it, then we won't practice discipline or membership or real discipleship. Neglecting church discipline is no problem, even if it's reckless, because, we think, "isn't God reckless?" Excommunication is not "loving," we're told. Love is "reckless," so say popular praise songs. It's not steadfast and certainly doesn't "visit iniquity" on anyone.

If people like to think of God as the kind of god who saves them even if they don't repent, they're like a woman with "pseudocyesis." She thinks she has a baby even when she doesn't. Biblical standards, like a sonogram, show no life is there, but they self-identify as a saint. So they believe, like the world, that everyone, especially pastors, are supposed to encourage them in their self-identity, their delusion. They think they have nothing to fear. They're sure no judgment will be visited on them, even if they haven't lived for God. They even mimic some of the signs of being a true saint. They can produce almost all the symptoms of spiritual life except the actual life. They're sure of it and will saunter up to the judgment seat saying, "Lord, Lord, look what I did for you" (like the "many" in Matthew 7:22.) They think that way because they have a wrong view of God. How do you like to think about God?

Worship Differently

When Moses saw Aaron's opinion of God, in the form of the golden calf, he smashed it. When he heard God's revelation of himself, he bowed his head and worshipped. He stood in awe of this transcendent, eternal, absolute God. Then he pleaded for mercy. He knew his people needed mercy. He didn't think they were adorable little darlings and if God had a problem with them it must be a problem with God. He didn't dare make up a cute saying, trying to win the Israelites over with a view of God that they would find too attractive to resist. He pleaded for mercy, aware of his sin; grieved by Israel's sin, of our need to have our sins dealt with before we can be accepted by a holy God.

When I was in High School an adult leader of a youth group told us that God doesn't get angry. He probably thought he was doing God a favor by saying that, making God look more attractive so we would be more willing to follow Him. That's how we like to think of God: an indulgent, hand-wringing god who kind of wistfully — somewhat desperately — hopes we'll come back to Him. So, we shape worship services to sentimentally beg people to come. But if we believe in this God, a kind and patient God, yes, but also a holy, sovereign God, who rules; who pardons but allows no sin to go unpunished, who loves and covenants, if that's the God we believe in, we will live differently. We will do church differently. We'll worship differently. Perhaps, we'll worship — really reverently worship — for the first time at all.

PILLAR 3

Knowing the Gospel

Romans 1:16–17

ONE OF THE MOST valuable people today in the business world is the effective salesman. Sales — or marketing — is perhaps the most prized talent in today's economy. In developed economies like ours, with a saturation in the market of products and services, what it takes for one company to succeed is the ability to sell its product. You can have the best restaurant or widget-maker in the world but if you aren't able to get other people to see that then your business is in trouble. Marketing is the key to survival in today's business world.

According to two separate business gurus, the first key to effective marketing is to "Understand your product" or "Know your stuff." One says, "This means having extensive product knowledge." Essentially, to be a good salesman, you have to be something of an expert on what you are selling. No one wants to buy a car from some guy who knows no more about cars than where to put the gas.

Some purists will squirm at the thought, but the truth is that the church is, in some ways, in the business of marketing. Oh, some will cry, "No we're not, we're just about obeying Jesus." Ok.

But the Lord Jesus told us in the Great Commission to do some marketing. After all, we can't obey Jesus' command to go and make disciples if we're not trying to persuade them to buy — with their lives — what we're offering.

Today there are many church leaders who are bold and innovative and successful at marketing. But what I often wonder, when I see the church and the gospel marketed, is whether they know what they are marketing. Sure, they know how to sell. But often they don't appear to know what they are supposed to be selling. They can attract people to their churches but do they know what a church is supposed to be? They can gather people to hear them speak but do they know what the gospel is?

The first tip on effective marketing is to know your product. The third pillar of a biblical church is that it knows and proclaims the gospel.

What Is the Gospel?

The word in Greek is *euangelion* which simply means "good news." It's not a special, technical term. It literally just means "good news." If you get a letter from the IRS saying that you are getting a big refund, that's good news. If you have a tumor, it's good news — gospel — if the doctors find it is benign, no threat. If you take a legal problem to a lawyer, he might give you good news — gospel — that it is minor; he can clear it up with little expense. If you check the sports news, you might find gospel — good news — that your team won.

So that is the name for the core Christian message: it is the Good News. That, right there, is a brilliant marketing technique: a name for our product that is immediately attractive. If it was called "imputed justification," that would be a harder sell. But it's called "good news." You can put that on a bumper sticker. But "good news" about what?

Many people today think the good news is that we are okay and if we can just feel okay, we'll start living better and everything will be okay. Some think the gospel is about Jesus being our example. If we can only be just like Him, we have accepted the gospel. For them, it's like a Buddhist eight-fold path or like Taoism, follow this way, this *tao*. Some think the gospel is a life-guard yelling out to a drowning man: "Take hold of the life preserver!" Some think the gospel is "God is love." That's a biblical idea (1 John 4:8). We hear it a lot. But how come we rarely hear the verse "Our God is a consuming fire" (Heb. 12:29)? Some think the gospel is just a new message of peace instead of the old message of vengeance. "Make love not war." Of course, what you get if you follow that is a bunch of kids making war on each other! All of these are, at best, half-gospels. A half-gospel masquerading as the whole gospel is no gospel at all.

What, then, is the whole truth about the gospel? To answer that question let's take apart Romans 1:16–17, phrase by phrase. We see three unfolding reasons, each signified by the word "for," or "because." First, Paul tells us why he is eager to preach the gospel in Rome. Then second, he tells us why he is not ashamed of the gospel. Then, finally, he tells us why it is the power of God for salvation. Through these three unfolding whys, he answers our big what: What is the gospel?

Why Paul Is Eager to Preach the Gospel in Rome

Paul begins Romans 1:16 with "for," or "because." That tells us that this sentence flows from, and explains what came just before. In verse 15, he wrote that he is eager to preach the gospel in Rome. Why? "Because" he's not ashamed of the gospel. We should be eager to preach the gospel, to evangelize, to tell people about it, to invite people to church where they'll hear the gospel, to expose our kids to it, to help with our church's evangelistic programs because we're not ashamed of it.

But is that not odd? Why would anyone be ashamed of the gospel? After all, we think of the gospel as a good thing, something to be proud of. If something is certainly true, it is "gospel truth." A popular style of music is "gospel music." Who would anyone be ashamed of the gospel? Actually, a lot more people would be if they knew what it was.

At the next verse after our text, Romans 1:18, Paul begins to describe exactly what the gospel is with startling arguments. He starts describing the "good news" by describing the "wrath of God" and the sins of men. He continues this theme for two entire chapters, concluding with a machine gun like spray of quotes from the book of Psalms, "There is no one righteous, not even one."

But these are hard-to-sell truths in our day. We like to think of ourselves as well-meaning people with a cuddly God. This affects how we "sell" the gospel and the church. I once attended a conference on church planting at which a speaker said that the church he planted was built on the principle that people, deep down, want God, they just don't know anything about Him. So, then, the church only needs to provide the knowledge of the God these people really, in their hearts, desire. Selling the church should be easy: just tell them about the God they don't know but will naturally love. The barely hidden implication: if your church isn't growing, it's because you're not marketing it right.

The problem with that approach is that that is exactly the opposite of what Romans 1 says. Romans 1:19 says, "For what can be known about God is plain to them, because God has shown it to them." God has made it known so that our conscience and nature makes God known. So it is not that people don't know anything about God. It's that they hate God. In verse 30, it says people are "God haters." They are sinners. It's true the good news is that God, through Jesus, saves people from their sins. But just telling people that they can be saved from their sins is like a doctor coming up to a person who thinks he's in perfect health and says, "Good news, I can cure your cancer." The problem is that he doesn't know, and will not accept the idea, that he has cancer. And, what's worse, he hates the doctor!

Now, this puts the church in an unusual position. First, the good news begins with the bad news that we are sinners. The world is offended by it. It doesn't want to be told it is sinful, just like no one wants to hear they have cancer. So from a marketing point of view, we're trying to sell something that we know most of our customers don't want. That means that the gospel is going to be a hard sell. And we can't change the product.

If people suddenly stop liking Coke, the Coca-Cola corporation will just change its product. It will do whatever it takes to survive in the business world. But if we do that — if we change the message or the church — just because it makes us more popular and more prosperous, we're in trouble. The world might like a little religion but it hates God so if we shape our church, our worship service, and especially our message merely to win friends, to bring in the crowds, we would have allowed people who hate God to dictate to us how to live and "worship." That's our dilemma: we have a product that people don't naturally want but we can't change the product. What are we to do?

In 1 Corinthians Paul said the gospel was foolishness to the Greeks, that is the Gentile world. They scoffed at it. It was hard to market this message to the Gentiles, the non-Jews. They didn't believe they were sinners needing salvation, they thought they just needed ethics, knowledge, and discipline. It was a hard sell. Now Paul plans on going to the capital city, the epitome of worldly power, and right in the belly of the beast proclaim this gospel they found so offensive. Yet he says, "I am not ashamed."

Times have changed but we seemed to have come full circle. Today we are surrounded by a culture that doesn't want to hear it is sinful, depraved, "dead in your trespasses and sins" (as Paul puts it in Ephesians 2). Oh, they may admit they need morality, improvement, education, after all, nobody is perfect, right? Maybe they even need enlightenment (like in Buddhism) or to follow the right path, to be a good family-member (like in Confucianism) or master the techniques that give power, like in Taoism. But salvation, resurrection from spiritual death, that's not something they feel they need. Dead people don't feel anything, not even their need for life. Even worse is the suggestion that God is angry with them in their sins, that there is such a thing as the "wrath of God" that needs to be satisfied. Talk about an unmarketable idea! So the temptation today, just as in Paul's day, is to be ashamed of the gospel, or at least of parts of it. Ashamed that we have to mention sin and judgment and the anger of God, that faith in Jesus is the only way. In that embarrassment, we are tempted to hide the hard-to-sell truths. But here, in Paul's first unfolding reason, he says he's not embarrassed by any of it.

Why He Is Not Ashamed of the Gospel

Why isn't he embarrassed? "For it is the power of God for salvation." Unbelievers will scoff, but Paul says he's not embarrassed because as ridiculous as it sounds to them, in this "good news" — beginning with such hard-to-market ideas — is the power of God. This then answers our question: What do we do with a product that people naturally don't want but we can't change.

What we need is some power that is capable of changing what people like; some kind of power that can transform people's hearts so that the God they used to hate they will now love. Paul, in Romans 1:16, says that the gospel contains that power, the "power of God for salvation." Notice three things about this: the source, the significance, and the salvation.

First, that the power is of God means God is the source. The power is in God and his gospel. We can't control it with the right prayer, the right formula, the right program, that right invitation hymn, the right revival meeting that will be sure to bring salvation.

A lot of what we find in the new marketing of the church — advertising, salesmanship, showmanship, social-media hype, manipulation, fog machines and lighting, all the same techniques we can employ to get people to buy something — doesn't have the power of God. Without the gospel, they have no power to get people to love the God they naturally hate. But the old ways are just as empty of power: moralism, ritualism (doing the right rituals, like baptism), legalism, even legalism with very low standards like we have a lot of today. People are told that the power is in us, in our will-power, our choices, our religion; our power is enough; that we, by the power in us, can live up to a standard of righteousness.

When the 19th century evangelist Charles Finney began preaching a gospel like that — that we had within us the power to change ourselves and make ourselves love God and righteousness — at least he had very high standards. He would rebuke people by name from the pulpit for loving luxury, wearing too expensive clothes, and the like. He believed that with the right preaching, the manipulation of the "anxious bench," the right formula of practices, he can manage the power of salvation. Now in our day, too many still have the same assumption: that the power to change is in us. But we've lowered the standards. Like not being a mass murderer. We have a lot of legalism now but it's legalism with low standards. The problem is the same: the belief that the power to change and repent and have faith is in us; the source is our will. But the power is "of God." He is the source.

Second, it is the "power" of God. If anyone is in Christ he is a new creature (2 Corinthians 5:17). The gospel is not just a few facts about Jesus that if you agree to, then we have accepted the gospel, even if our life shows no change. That the gospel is the power of God, means that when it comes into our life, it makes a significant impact. The power of God makes us new. That will definitely show in the way we live.

Third, it is power for salvation. Romans 1:17 ends by quoting from Habakkuk 2:4, that those who are right with God shall live. They will be raised up from death, resurrected, new. The gospel has the power to rescue people from their sin, from death, for a right relationship with God, for life. The righteous will live by their faith.

Who is the gospel for? Romans 1:16–17 says it is the power of God for the salvation for "everyone who believes." It's not for everyone. It's not for those who do not believe. Salvation is revealed "from faith to faith." We are right with God through faith. That is, faith is the means, the way, salvation comes through to those who the gospel is for. Then salvation builds up our faith. It is "to faith."

Martin Luther defined faith as "a living, daring confidence in God's grace, so sure and certain that a man would stake his life on it a thousand times." Faith is the way salvation is shown or manifest to us. That's what the "revealed" means. Our faith demonstrates that we are saved. It's not what we muster up to save ourselves. Salvation is expressed by the fact that now, we who were once God-hating unbelievers, are God-loving believers. Our salvation is manifest — demonstrated — by the fact that we now have a living, daring confidence in God's grace, so sure and certain that we would stake our life on it a thousand times.

Salvation, then, comes to us through faith. But here we have a problem: If we are as bad as the Bible says we are, how can we do something as perfectly good as believing God? How can we have a living, daring confidence in God's grace, if we are God-hating people who are dead in our sins? Belief, faith in God, is the best "work" you could ever do. But if we are as dead in sin as the Bible says we are, how can we have the "life" it takes to have that kind of faith in God?

We need power! We need power to believe, power to change dead hearts of stone into living hearts of flesh. Paul says he's not ashamed of the gospel because it has that power. In it is the power to save you, even to give you the faith you couldn't muster up on your own. Paul here writes that the power of God for salvation is for everyone who believes. Notice that it doesn't say people are saved because they believe. Rather, it says God's power is "for" — that is, working on behalf of — those who believe. Notice, first, what he doesn't say. He doesn't say what many people today assume he says. He doesn't say that we believe — that we muster up the faith all on our own — and that makes it possible to access the power of God for our use; that somehow we provide the key of faith that unlocks God's power. Remember, people "dead in sin" are not going to believe God.

Positively, what does Paul mean? He means that the power of God enables us to believe in the first place. The reason why a believer has the power to believe is because God's power is at work "for" him. But we like to think we've done something for ourselves. I've heard this analogy used for the relationship between faith and salvation: we are drowning, weighed down by sin, sinking into hell. But then Jesus comes along and throws out the life-preserver. The life-preserver is the gospel. The proclamation of the gospel is the good news to drowning people, "Hey, there's a life-preserver. Reach out and grab it!" We have to do our part by taking hold of it. That's faith, they say, taking hold of the life-preserver. There are some good things about that analogy. We do have to believe. Like in the analogy, faith is not just a feeling. Faith takes hold of something. It grasps the gospel and doesn't let go. At least this analogy gets something important about faith: that faith is like a clenched hand on a life-preserver and faith can't be in anything we want it to be in. Faith has to be in the right thing. If you're drowning at sea and you grab a shark, instead of a life preserver, drowning will be the least of your worries! Just like you have to grab the right thing, faith has to be in the right thing. It has to be in Christ, in the true Jesus of the gospel. He's the One we hold onto with our faith.

However, the problem with the life-preserver analogy is that the Bible doesn't say we are merely in danger of potentially drowning, that sin is just weighing us down but we're still alive fighting for life. It says we are "dead" in our sins and trespasses (Eph. 2:1). We're not a drowning man waving his arms desperately asking for help. We're a pale corpse floating face down in the water. Jesus doesn't just throw us a life-preserver and leave it up to us to save ourselves by taking hold of it. He jumps in and he takes hold of us. He drags us to shore and breathes life into us. Jesus saves.

So, in the gospel, salvation is not merely made available by God. It is not merely offered, like the way a grocer offers milk for sale. It is effected. The gospel is not merely potential power, that we unlock with our techniques: saying the right prayer, doing the right ritual, living by the right morality. No. It is real power, the power of God for salvation. Do you really want to know what the gospel is? It is so simple you can reduce it to a bumper sticker: "Jesus saves!"

He doesn't merely throw out the life-preserver and leave it up to us to "exercise our faith" and so contribute our little bit to saving ourselves. The gospel is that Jesus saves. Hebrews 12:2 says that "Jesus is the founder — or some versions have "author" — and perfecter of our faith." Our faith is founded by Him, not by our sin-enslaved will; it is authored by Him, just as a writer sits down before a blank sheet of paper, or computer screen, and authors a book. It originates from Him. The paper or computer can't take credit for the book an author writes. We can't even take credit for the faith God inspires in us. Salvation is, from beginning to end, all the work of God for the glory of God. As it says Romans 1:17 salvation is "from faith for faith."

The flip side of this is described by the Lord Jesus himself. In John 10:25–26, he tells the Pharisees, "You do not believe because you do not belong to my sheep." Think on that statement carefully. He doesn't say, "You do not belong to my sheep because you do not believe." That's what many people today expect the Lord Jesus to say. But he doesn't. He says that people don't believe because they are not his sheep. Belonging to God's flock is not dependent on believing. It's not a lack of faith that puts them outside of God's sheep. It's the other way around. Believing is dependent on being a sheep. Those who are sheep, believe. Sheep believe. It's what they do. They're not sheep because they believe. They believe because they are sheep. Belonging to God's flock — experiencing the transforming power of God — enables a person to believe.

This message of the power of God is "to the Jew first and also to the Greek." By "Greek" he means all non-Jewish people. The good news is not for one race or culture or nation and not for another. He is saying it is for all people, all kinds of people. The gospel by its nature allows for no discrimination, no isolating our proclamation to one group and ignoring all the others, no niche marketing. The gospel by its nature does not allow for racism or segregation, preferring just our kind of people. Being inter-racial is not just some cutting edge marketing technique for the new generation or some optional extra, our little distinction to set us apart in a competitive market. It is who we must be as a gospel believing church.

Why It Is the Power of God for Salvation

What is it about this good news that transforms us from God-hating wolves to God-loving sheep? Romans 1:17 begins "because in it —the gospel — the righteousness of God is revealed." First, what is the "righteousness of God?" Martin Luther wrote that he at first thought that this "righteousness of God" referred to a new moral standard. The Law had one moral standard, that was already hard enough. But then, he first believed, God brought the gospel and raised the standard even higher. As in the sermon on the Mount: you've heard that you aren't to commit murder. But now you shouldn't even hate. You've heard that you aren't to commit adultery. But now you can't lust. So he wrote that he first hated that term, "the righteousness of God." But then when studying this verse, it dawned on him that the "righteousness" here was not a new, higher standard that had to be met. Instead, it was a right relationship, being put right with God; what sin has done to alienate us from God and bring God's anger on us, God has wiped away (for everyone who believes.) He attributed Christ's perfect life to us while attributing our sins to Christ on the cross, so, in the words to that great song, "In Christ Alone," "the wrath of God was satisfied." When Luther realized this, he said, "the light of the gospel came into my soul, the gates of paradise opened, and I walked through."

Righteousness is being right with God, having a right relationship with him. The things that alienated you from God have been cleared away. So, now God is no longer angry with you. That good relationship is made known by the gospel.

What is the gospel? It's not, I'm ok, you're ok. That'll sell but it's not the gospel. It's not that we have the power within us. We just need to find the right technique, the right *tao*, or like mastering *feng shui*, arrange life to our advantage. The power is not in a technique. That's sold big but it's not the gospel. It is not a lifeguard telling a drowning man to take hold of the life-preserver. It's too late for that. We're already drowned. We're bobbing face down in the water, dead in our sins. The gospel is the good news that Jesus has the power to raise us to life. But it's good news that is impossible for us (alone) to market, even to believe, but the good news that has within it God's power to make us love it and love Him, to buy him with our lives. When you do, the light will come into your soul, the gates of paradise will open and you will walk through. Then you will know, the gospel is as simple as that two-word bumper sticker: Jesus saves!

PILLAR 4

Genuine Conversion

Luke 19:1–10

EVER KNOWN ANYONE WHOSE LIFE is a mess but who is certain he
or she is saved? I once worked with a very troubled man who was
the verge of a divorce. I don't know if he could say three words
without one of them being profane. I once suggested he go to
church and talk to his pastor, with the hope he would be converted.
He told me that he had already been saved and baptized when he
was 12. He was sure he had taken care of that need. He had been
given assurance.

My cousin claimed, "I've taken care of that." When we were
both about 16, walking together around Legion Field in Birming-
ham, outside an Alabama football game, I picked up a tract which
I began to read out-loud. It read something like, "Get the thing you
need the most." I paused. She asked, "What?" The tract continued,
"Jesus Christ as your Lord and Savior." She said, "Oh, I've taken
care of that already." Since then, she married a nominal Catholic;
later converted to Catholicism; later divorced, and soon remarried.
I asked what sort of wedding she had — Catholic or Protestant. I
was told she was married by a judge but it was sort of Protestant.
I've never seen any interest from her in spiritual things. But she's

probably still convinced that she had taken care of her salvation. Someone had given her assurance.

We have a religious movement around us that is what I call — since they call themselves this — "the Old Time Religion." The Old Time Religion — the OTR — does what we saw in the last chapter: sell the gospel. Except instead of getting people to buy it with their lives, it thinks all we must do is buy it with a "decision," a single act that then confers on us the status — many say the irrevocable status — of being converted, being "saved," they'd say. If you've made the decision, especially in the right environment, as the organ softly plays "Just As I Am" or as the Sunday School teacher leans on you to repeat a "sinner's prayer" (that they made up), then you are certainly "saved." You're converted, they assure you. You don't ever need to doubt it, no matter what you do with your life after that decision.

The goal of the OTR is to get you to make the decision. The decision is merely about what you will believe on some points of faith, not how you will live. If you make that decision, they give you assurance of salvation. You exchange a decision for the promise of eternal life. It seems like an offer you can't refuse. They dispense assurance of salvation like a Christmas parade throws out candy. Or like Oprah giving out cars: "You get assurance and you get assurance and you get assurance. Everybody gets assurance!"

The older — and biblical — message that good trees bear good fruit; that if you don't bear fruit in keeping with repentance, then you need, like Paul said to the Corinthians, to examine yourself as to whether you are really "in the faith" (2 Cor. 13:5), is lost in the OTR. The OTR doesn't understand that salvation makes you a new creature and that will definitely show, not in perfection, but in change. It doesn't tell people that a "decision" without the fruit of repentance is a counterfeit conversion. The result is sick churches, full of people, like my cousin or my former co-worker, who aren't really converted but are sure they are. They've been given assurance by people who don't clearly understand conversion. But a biblical church knows what genuine conversion is.

What is genuine conversion? We see one in Luke 19:1–10, the story of Zacchaeus, with three facets of genuine conversion: the call, the choice, and the change.

The Call

First, we see the call. Jesus' call is preeminent. Out of the crowd, Jesus called one man. Jesus takes the initiative. Jesus' call comes first. But some say that Zacchaeus showed his faith when he climbed up the tree, that he was moving to Jesus, doing his part. But Luke 19:3 simply says that "he was seeking to see who Jesus was." If Tom Cruise came to my town, if he walked down Main Street where I live, I would probably be interested enough to go out to take a look. I'd be curious. I'd like to be able to say that I've seen Tom Cruise in person. That doesn't mean I want to follow Tom Cruise or I believe in what he says. He's a good actor but spiritually he's goofy, a Scientologist. But I might want to see him. That desire to see would even be stronger in their day when you could hear about someone but never have seen a picture of them. That's all that Luke tells us about what Zacchaeus does here. When interpreting this passage, it's important not to read into it what is not there.

The only reason it tells us why Zacchaeus climbed the tree is because he is short and wanted to see Jesus. It doesn't tell us he was seeking to follow Jesus. But it does tell us that Jesus took the initiative. The Lord Jesus stopped. Jesus called out to Zacchaeus. Jesus invited himself over for a meal. Not reading anything into this passage, it tells us that, at least in this salvation, Jesus is the active one. He's the One who acts first.

Here, he calls Zacchaeus. Of all the people in that crowd, Jesus chooses the most unlikely, a man who collaborated with the Roman occupiers, an outcast from the rest of society. But Jesus called him. "Come down." That caused people to murmur against Jesus.

This is the way the gospel is. Martin Luther insisted that whenever the gospel is clearly proclaimed, controversy would surely follow. It does here. The people "murmur." Jesus is breaking their mores. They had ostracized Zacchaeus and people like him to punish them for breaking God's law. It's not as though Jesus is always opposed to ostracism. This is not a story about "breaking down barriers," about including everyone, regardless of their lifestyle, about not being judgmental. In fact, Jesus tells the church, in Matthew 18:17 to treat a believer who continues to live in sin just like the Jews were treating Zacchaeus. He says we're supposed to regard an unrepentant brother as a "pagan or a tax collector." Zacchaeus is a tax collector. So, in theory, there's nothing necessarily wrong with how Jewish society was treating Zacchaeus. Nevertheless, he was Jesus' choice. Jesus takes the initiative and calls him and chooses him.

The Choice

That Jesus first chose Zacchaeus doesn't mean that Zacchaeus doesn't choose too. Some think that when we talk about Jesus calling first, about predestination, we're saying that we don't choose. That's wrong. We do choose. We choose because he chooses us first. What's the difference between genuine and counterfeit conversion? The genuine begins with Jesus calling and that call results in us choosing. In Luke 19:1–10, Zacchaeus hears the call. Jesus says he must stay with him. It is necessary for Jesus to fulfill his mission to stay with this out-cast.

Then comes the choice. Zacchaeus hears Jesus' call, hurries down from the tree, delighted that Jesus has called him. The call creates joy in his heart. This is the way it is with the Lord's call. When he effectively and personally calls you, it's not as though he drags you kicking and screaming to do something or go somewhere you don't want to go. His call creates your choice. You receive him with joy. His call inspires in you the ability and desire to choose Him. Once called, you'll hurry to choose Him.

So Jesus is the guest of a sinner. The people grumble. Of course, he would be a guest of a sinner no matter who he decides to eat with, even the strictest Pharisee. But they don't know that. They believe that they are not sinners if they are trying to keep the law. It's those people who think they are not sinners, who are assured that they are fine with God despite not being changed, who are in the most danger. The one who knows he's a sinner, is singled out for salvation.

This is our problem today: We have handed out assurance of salvation to people who have not shown the evidence of change. Because they are now assured, in their minds, that they are saved, they don't think they need salvation. They think that's taken care of. They think their biggest need is for a relationship or money or beer. They are sure. But there is such a thing as false assurance.

The Change

Are you sure of your salvation? If so, why? In other words, how do you know? Because of your doctrinal opinions? No, because of a change. Notice how Luke tells us Zacchaeus repents. How do we know that Zacchaeus repents? Because he reports how sorry he felt? Because he cried? Because he prayed the right prayer? Luke didn't write at all about Zacchaeus' inward feelings, not even about some "sinner's prayer." Luke doesn't even tell us he repents. Luke shows us he repents. Zacchaeus' repentance is demonstrated in his actions. So repentance isn't a mere emotion of sorrow, although it definitely produces that. It is a root cause of observable behavior. In other words, repentance shows itself; it can be seen.

You've seen those "before and after" photos of people on diets; before they were fat and after they are skinny. Repentance is like that. Before you are living one way, after you are living another way. You can take a picture of the difference. If the emotion of sorrow doesn't lead to photographable changes, then it is not true repentance. It's just a feeling.

This is vital for us to understand for a biblical church today because there is, in the OTR, an omission of repentance. There is a theology of "cheap grace," easy-believism. In this theology, one can be a Christian but not really have Jesus as Lord. Faith is defined as accepting a few facts about Jesus. But it's a faith that is like the way I believe in Australia. I believe there is an Australia; I have no reason to doubt it; I even have a friend, Iain, who says he lives in Australia. Sometimes I get messages from Iain claiming he's in Australia. But the existence of Australia has no impact on my life. It hasn't changed me. If I find out that there really is no Australia, that it was really all made up by the US National Park Service to hide the fact that they have a unique collection of strange animals, my life won't change a bit. The doctrine of Australia makes no impact on my life.

That's what some people think believing in Jesus for salvation is: just agree that he died for our sins, that he rose from the dead, that He's somehow related to God. Believe that, they say, and the deal is done. You'll go to heaven. And some think, "Why not? I have nothing to lose. I'll say I agree with those facts. I have no reason not to. I'll repeat a prayer and, voila!, I'm 'saved.' I've taken care of that. Now, where's the best bar for picking up girls?!" You might even know someone like that.

But we see here the idea that one can be a genuine Christian and not experience a radical change, that one can merely agree with certain facts about Jesus and supposedly be saved is a false idea. The common belief, today, that between Christians and the lost is a third category of so-called "carnal Christians" who are really saved — because they don't disagree with the facts but whose lives are not marked by repentance and faith, is a false doctrine. It's a cover up for an unbiblical doctrine of conversion. It can be a dangerous cover-up. When you combine the idea of a "carnal Christian," with a false idea that faith is just intellectually agreeing with a few basic facts about Jesus, and then "once-saved-always-saved," you get unsaved people who earnestly believe they have taken care of their salvation, who are told they are saved by churches, who are included as church members no matter what their lives say, and who testify to the world that being saved is absolutely worthless.

How do we know we're genuinely converted, then? Is it because of our morality and manners and knowledge? Look at the rich young ruler (just 12 verses before this in Luke 18:18–30). The rich young ruler was devout, kept the law externally, appeared sincere, respected Jesus and asked him the right questions, and even could feel sorrow about his unwillingness to obey Jesus. He'd probably be considered a model church member in many places today. That he wasn't willing to go 100% into following Jesus just means he's a bit of a "carnal Christian," they'd say. Remember he's already got morality, and religion, not to mention money and power. He's not a hypocrite like the Pharisees, out to destroy Jesus. So he's decent, religious, earnest, and has been that way for all his life. In our day, we might be surprised that such a man is even questioning his salvation. The OTR would almost certainly give him assurance. But the truth is that he is not converted; he experienced no radical, inward change. For the rich young ruler the Lord Jesus made it precisely clear what kind of change was expected of him. He was supposed to liquidate all his assets, give them to the poor, and become one of the disciples. That would have been a photographable change brought about in his life. True conversion produces change. It did in Zacchaeus' life. It would have in the ruler's life.

The rich young ruler and Zacchaeus are opposites. The only thing they have in common is that they are both rich. But the rich ruler is justly rich. Zacchaeus used his power to bilk money out of the powerless. The rich ruler was a respected leader, admired and accepted. Zacchaeus was an out-cast. But it was Zacchaeus who heard Jesus with joy. The rich ruler received Jesus' call with regret, and went away. He was too attached to his money. If the rich ruler believed that giving away his wealth and following Jesus would give him "treasure in heaven" he would have thought nothing of it. He would have decided to follow Jesus, no turning back. If he had faith it would have produced repentance — its conjoined twin virtue — and he would have turned and followed Jesus. Zacchaeus did. Notice, for both, repentance is shown by how they handle their money. If your faith makes no impact on your check-book, we have reason to question whether it's real. The rich young ruler didn't have faith. So there is no change. Zacchaeus did and so gave.

My co-worker who was troubled and always profane was a Baptist. I know someone else who is very faithful and considerate, as committed to her family as anyone could be. She's moral, dutiful, faithful, helpful and kind. But I know she's not a Christian because she is a Buddhist. She's my mother-in-law. She is a "good," moral person who will faithfully sacrifice to her ancestors. That's the way she was raised and, so far, she doesn't want to change. She has lived most of her life in Singapore. Now, imagine if she were born and raised in a small town in the American Bible-belt. She would almost certainly be a church member somewhere. She'd be faithful too; she'd be the type who comes for every meeting, cooks for the pot-luck dinners, stays after to clean up and volunteers where needed. She would be a pillar of the church. She might even make a "decision" at the right time. Now hopefully with all that church attendance she might someday genuinely encounter God's grace. But perhaps she wouldn't. After all, decisions are not necessarily conversions.

There's nothing we human beings can do to guarantee that God will save anyone. As Jesus said in John 3, we must be "born of the Spirit" and then he says that "the Spirit blows where he will." He is sovereign; we can't control Him; we can't corner him and make him save people who say a certain prayer. So this faithful lady might go her whole life in church and not really be saved. Just like the rich ruler was moral and religious — even went to Jesus seeking counsel — but wasn't saved. If we think of salvation as just a combination of "easy-believism" — "cheap grace" — and a moral life, we'd almost be certain she was a true Christian. We'd give her assurance.

Now, let's change her sex. Let's say she's a man, a "he" not a "she." He responds as a child to one of those emotional invitations, one of those manipulative kinds that first asks the person to raise his hand, then stand up, and then come forward and say a prayer and is then told he is saved. But maybe he's not really saved. But he's given assurance. Being the responsible, dutiful type, he feels an obligation to go to church. Like before, he's a pillar of the church. Maybe he's successful in business and gives, tithes. He'll probably soon be made deacon, if he's in a Baptist church (the functional equivalent, in their traditional polity, of an elder). He'll have great influence on the direction of the church. Or maybe at another meeting, as a young man, he's manipulated into giving his life to "full time Christian service." So he goes to seminary and becomes a pastor. But if his faith is just "easy-believism" plus morality he might never have really encountered the grace of God. Which means, according to Romans 1, he is someone who "hates God"; that he is, according to Ephesians 2, "dead in trespasses and sin." Now he's leading the church. That's how churches die.

Salvation Has Come

How do we know that Zacchaeus is saved? Notice how Jesus puts it in Luke 19:9. "Today salvation has come to this house." There's a double meaning here. He's not merely saying that Zacchaeus was saved. He said, "Salvation has come." Jesus' name means, "The Lord is salvation." He is the Lord, and so he is salvation. So, quite literally, He, Salvation, came to that house.

He's also saying something important about salvation. Think about the way this is put: "salvation has come." How would you describe this event? If it were me, my usual way of saying it would be, "Zacchaeus got saved." That's our normal expression. It sounds as if Zacchaeus did the work himself, that he's the active one, the subject of the verb. Our idiom sounds as if salvation were out there for the taking and Zacchaeus went out and got some for himself, like we talk about getting milk at the store. But that's our way of saying things. Jesus says it differently. "Salvation has come to this house." In Jesus' way, salvation is active. Zacchaeus didn't go out and get himself salvation. Salvation went out and got Zacchaeus. Salvation, Jesus himself, is the active one. Zacchaeus isn't the subject; he's the object. Remember the gospel: Jesus saves. That's what he did to Zaccahaeus.

He emphasizes this again in Luke 19:10, Jesus' mission statement: "The Son of Man came to seek and to save what was lost." He doesn't say he came only to seek and invite the lost. He didn't come only to make salvation possible; merely to hope the lost respond positively to the offer of salvation; to make it available, like a store makes milk available, but leaves it up to the lost whether they want to get some or not. He came to seek them out, as Jesus does here, and save them, as Jesus does here.

Why did the Lord Jesus call Zacchaeus? He says that Salvation has come to Zacchaeus because he is a son of Abraham. What does he mean? Is he just saying that he's Jewish so he gets saved? Obviously not. Probably everyone in that crowd was Jewish, descendants of Abraham whom Jesus did not bring salvation to. The rich young ruler was a son of Abraham, literally speaking, but he wasn't saved. So what does he mean?

In John 8:39 Jesus told the Pharisees, that you are not sons of Abraham. They were physical descendants but did not have the faith of Abraham. Zacchaeus did. You couldn't tell it by looking at his life up until this point. But God knows those who are His. That's why he stopped in front of the tree, surrounded by literal children of Abraham, but looked up and saw in the tree a true, spiritual son of Abraham. So Jesus called him. As Jesus says in John 10:27, "My sheep hear my voice."

Finally, the Lord Jesus explains why all this happened. Because, he says in verse 10, he came, to seek and to save the lost. That's his purpose. This is his mission statement, as clear and as bold as it could possibly be: to seek and save (not just invite, not just to beg but to effectively save) the lost. It's not to teach church kids how to be well-mannered, well-dressed, well-adjusted, successful people. It's not for our entertainment. It's not to mobilize us for politics. It's to seek and to save the lost.

Three Applications

First, adopt the Lord's mission. If seeking and saving the lost is the mission of Jesus, it better be ours. A biblical church has the same mission the Lord has. Evangelism is a pillar of a biblical church. That means that we should encourage those gifted in one-on-one evangelism to use that gift. That means that churches should have programs that allow members who may not be gifted in one-on-one evangelism to play a part in evangelism, a program that reaches people outside the church, like children and presents the gospel to them. That means that our prayer meetings — and our private prayers — had better have more to do with fulfilling that mission than anything else (like health). Adopt Jesus' priorities, that his mission is ours. That means we be willing to sacrifice every secondary goal — to be big or respectable or just comfortable — for that mission.

Since we're the Body of Christ, our mission should be the same as Christ's: to seek and save the lost. My wife and I attended a Presbyterian church plant, which we couldn't be members of because of our stance on baptism but we wanted to help it grow. We regularly brought to their Sunday School three children of a heroin addict. One Sunday when we had to be away, we asked a member of that church to pick up those three kids. She declined, citing insurance. I don't believe that car insurance will penalize you for picking up kids for Sunday School but even if it does and your mission is to seek and save the lost, you'll pick up the tab. No one in the church was interested in bringing those three needy kids to church. Sadly, but not surprisingly, the church collapsed. The church plant failed. They hadn't adopted the Lord's mission.

Our church, early on, could have bought a traditional church building, with pews. Or we could have bought a gym, with basketball markings on the floor. We can use a traditional building for church meetings but that's all. We can use a gym for church meetings and for drawing kids to evangelistic programs. We chose the gym because we're called to carry on the mission of seeking and saving the lost. Like Jesus, we have to be willing to withstand the grumbling of those who think we should be spending our time with "better" people, the kind who like pews. Evangelism is a priority.

Secondly, adapt to the biblical reality that when salvation comes into your life, it will make a change, a change you can photograph, you can see in your check-book, a change you will receive with great joy, like Zacchaeus. We have made a mistake in too quickly and too freely telling people — people like the rich ruler, or worse, even just some young kid who responds to an emotional invitation — that now he's taken care of his salvation. Now that we see what genuine salvation is, how are we supposed to say that a small child is genuinely converted? He or she may be but how do we know? That means that baptism is for disciples, people who show with their life that they are converted. It means that church discipline is also a pillar of a biblical church so that we take away assurance of salvation when someone's life denies it.

Genuine conversion is shown in giving. The rule of Christian giving is not a tithe but generosity. How much is "generous"? If the first question your mind goes to is looking for a minimum you can get away with, then there is a problem. What man is really in love with his wife and the first thing that comes to his mind, whenever he thinks about their wife, is "Do I have to be sexually faithful to her? Is that a burden I really have to bear?" I don't see how we go from the Old Testament rule, which was 10% (from Abraham and Jacob in Genesis who gave a tithe when God gave to them), to a rule that is "generous," and the percentage goes down? How does that work? How does "generous" become less than what used to be the minimum required? We should be able to see the change your conversion has wrought by your giving to your church.

Finally, be adept at reaching out, like Jesus did here, in a way that is attractive to them; be adept at challenging hypocrites who think they've taken care of salvation when their life isn't changed and be adept at examining ourselves: devoutness, church forms, morality, does not necessarily indicate conversion; conversion involves a total change of allegiance. Jesus is Lord. It's not enough just to be conservative and moral, like the rich ruler. We need to believe the Lord Jesus; we need faith. If we have faith, we'll also have repentance. That's why one of the best signs of having been truly converted is a tender-heartedness, a heart that is happily adept at changing.

Are you sure you're saved? If so, why? Because you're moral and religious? Because you said the right prayer? Because you needed salvation and so went out and got it, like getting milk at a store? Or did Salvation go out and get you? Remember, we can't concoct a religion, a prayer, an atmosphere that will ensure that you get saved. Salvation must act. So pray. Pray passionately for Salvation to visit; for Jesus, to call you, to choose you, and to change you.

PILLAR 5

Meaningful Membership

Hebrews 10:19–25

I LIVED ABOUT 15 MINUTES from Punxsutawney, Pennsylvania, the home of "Phil" the groundhog to whom we look, every February 2nd, to see if we'll have six more weeks of winter. It was a cute little, unofficial, non-holiday that most people only paid some amused attention to, a few minutes once a year, until the movie Ground Hog Day came out in 1993. Since then "Ground Hog Day" hs become a by-word for futility, for no matter what you do, nothing changes. It's about a weather man who gets caught in a loop, re-experiencing Ground Hog Day over and over again. No matter what he does nothing changes. That's what I feel addressing church membership is like. No matter how many scriptures one uses to show its importance (like Matthew 18:15–17, much of 1 Corinthians or, especially, Hebrews 10:19–25), some continue to believe that the church is simply their individual service provider, like their favorite restaurant, to be changed for whatever reason you want.

A pious-sounding lady once said, "I know who I belong to." It sounds so spiritual. "I know who I belong to." That was her reason for abandoning the church she had covenanted to be a member.

She had exclaimed that she'd never leave church #1 unless God spoke to her directly. That resolve lasted a few months until she decided that she could have a weekly family reunion if she went to church #2. She quickly abandoned that church to go back to an old church, #3, because the pastor was a friend. When that didn't work out, she found a church #4 — and counting — which she now piously calls her "church family." She thinks that because she belongs to Christ, she doesn't need to belong to a specific church. Her commitment to any particular church can be broken on a whim. If you ask her why she's leaving, she says, "I know who I belong to." In the meantime, she also left her husband. Apparently, she didn't belong to him either. For me or you to tell her that she should not merely go to church but be a covenanted member of a specific church, would be like a restaurant owner berating a former customer for not coming to the restaurant regularly anymore. No one expects loyalty to a restaurant. Why should they expect it to a church? That's many people's idea of the church.

We live in a culture soaked in individualism. They say if you want to know about water, the last one to ask is a fish. And so if you want to know about individualism, the last one to ask is an American. We are swimming in its acids. That's why addressing church membership to many Americans is like Ground Hog Day. No matter what you do, the next day you'll be back where you started. That acid has soaked its way into the church so that when the instruction is done about covenanting to be a member of a particular body, the next day the American wakes up and he's a self-seeking consumer again. A church member, in the Bible-belt, could unashamedly say, "I know who I belong to," as an excuse to abandon the people she had said she belonged to. That's the acids of individualism dissolving the church.

Many churches' response to that church-as-restaurant attitude is to admit it. Surrender to it. Enable it. They admit it by accepting the reality of it; not asking attenders to become members, to enter into covenant with one another; letting covenant-breakers, without rebuke, go their merry way; and then spend their time marketing the church to these people. They busily market themselves to their former customers to get them to come back for a visit. A gospel sing gives them an excuse to invite them. "You'll love it; don't miss it!" Or maybe a revival or a "home-coming." Above all, don't offend them on their way out, by telling them that they're breaking their commitment, because then they won't come back. Besides, we can't rebuke them (we often think) because we recognize that they're right: they belong to Christ (not us — not the Body of Christ?); that we cannot interfere in the sacredness of their individual free choices about how to be a member; about whether they should actually keep their commitments; whether their "yes" should be yes; whether they should have integrity; whether they should keep their vows even if it hurts (Psalm 15:4); whether they should be expected to be a covenant-keeper like God; whether they should actually consider the impact of their decision on the other people in the church they are leaving behind.

So, many reason — since "I know who I belong to" — I could just stay home and watch my favorite preacher, all by myself in my living room, with none of those other annoying people to make me uncomfortable. Why not, if we don't belong to a specific body? During the pandemic, many churches encouraged this spectator-church mentality by speaking ironically of "joining us on-line." They tell people, "Do church online." They claim that there can be a "virtual church." If, for a brief time, the best a church can do is offer sermons and lessons via the internet, that's fine. But don't tell people that watching from home constitutes gathering, that one can "do church" — do assembly — without assembling. By doing that, churches are teaching that church is akin to a theater. If the cinemas are closed, or you just don't want the bother of going out, watch the newest movie by streaming from the comfort of your couch. After all, the only thing that matters is my entertainment. The virtual churches are encouraging the same attitude: "Entertain me or leave me alone but above all . . . I know who I belong to and it isn't you (church)."

That's the dominate idea of the church in America. The Bible's idea of the church is radically different than that: a vision of the church built and presided over by Christ as the family of

God (Galatians 6:10, 1 Timothy 3:15). You would no more leave your church because some slight thing, like the music, was better elsewhere than you would leave your family for another because the new family had more fun at family game night. In Hebrews 10:19–25, we see three commands to the church that require covenanted membership, a genuine church family, and are contrary to the church-as-theater, "virtual church" ethos: come together, hold together, and consider together.

Coming Together

At the root of I-know-who-I-belong-to-mentality is the assumption that we belong to Christ without belonging to his Body, his temple, his family. We're disconnected. Oh, we might get tips from each other on how to build up this relationship with Christ but, in the end, we're alone. No. Hebrews 10:19–25 shows us that our ability even to come to God, to approach our Father in heaven, is not just between individuals and God. It is based on what was done for us. Not for me and, by the way, maybe for you. But for us, corporately. What Christ did was for us, the family of God, the Body of Christ. He bought a church, not disparate individuals (Acts 20:28.)

In Hebrews 10:19 to 22, we see two foundations that have been laid for us, that all believers are founded on: first, we can now enter the presence of God by the blood of Jesus and, second, we have a great priest over the house of God. The blood of Jesus gives us confidence that we can enter God's presence. That blood was spilled when his body was broken, when it was torn, just like that curtain dividing the holy of holies, where the presence of God symbolically dwelled above the ark of the covenant, in the holy place, where only the priest could go. The old temple restricted access to the presence of God, prohibiting it to all but the high priest, the "great priest." Now, however, we can confidently come to God. That confidence is based not on my individualistic life, what I've done (or not done), "my" religion, but on what Jesus did for us all. So that way is the same for all God's people. We do not come to

God, as individuals, each in our own way. We come, all together, in the only way that has been provided, or we don't make it at all.

The advantage of that is that we can be confident. If we had to come by ourselves, on our own merits, we'd have to wonder if we'd done enough. Had we given enough or prayed enough or sacrificed enough. But because we come based on what Christ has done, we can be confident since Christ's life and death were perfect.

We come because we have a great priest (Hebrews 10:21). He is the "high priest" of not simply us as individuals; not like the way we may have the same cell-phone service, we just all happen to have AT&T, that gives us access to wireless communication. But that's all that joins us together, our checks go to the same company. No. We get to communicate, wirelessly, with God, because we're all part of the same group plan.

Jesus is the great priest over the "house of God." The comparison is to the temple. God lives in the temple, the church. Just as the high priests in the Old Testament were not the priests over individual bricks or planks or stones but over the whole temple, so Christ is the high priest over the God's temple, joined together with each part. A brick or stone or plank could not say to the brick or stone or plank next to it, "I know who I belong to. Butt out!" No. Every part joined together makes for the House of God. Over that Christ presides as the great priest. That is the biblical idea of the church.

With the rending of Christ's body making a way for us, we can confidently come together. "Let us draw near." But draw near to what? To God or to each other? First, he means to God. We have confidence to enter the holy place, the presence of God. We can know that our sins are covered. Have confidence even though we have individually sinned and the soul that sins shall die. Still, Christ's sacrifice for us pays for our sins; it appeases God's anger at our sins; it enables Christ's perfect life to be attributed to us so that when we approach the Father, he sees us just as if we had lived as perfectly as the Son. That's why we can be confident. Not because we're moral or religious or memorized our Bible books in order. Our individual lives are not confidence-inducing. But Jesus' is. It is trusting in him that can give us a "true heart in full assurance of faith." Our hearts can be sprinkled clean, with the blood of Jesus, from an evil conscience. We don't have to feel guilty and fearful of God because of our sins.

When Martin Luther was an especially strict monk, he was also nominated to become a priest, to have the privilege of saying the words they believed, in their theology, that would convert the simple bread and wine into the literal body and blood of Christ. That was, in their view, the way to draw near to God, through that sacrifice, called "the mass." But it had to be done over and over. As he stood saying his first mass thinking he was holding the real broken body of Jesus, declaring "This is the Body of Christ," he trembled and he reported later: "At these words, I was utterly stupefied and terror-stricken. I thought to myself "With what tongue shall I address such Majesty . . . ? Who am I, that I should lift up mine eyes or raise my hands to the divine Majesty? The angels surrounded Him. At his nod the earth trembles. And shall I, a miserable little pygmy, speak to the living, eternal and true God?" That's the lack of confidence, the "evil conscience" mentioned in Hebrews 10:22. But faith in the completed sacrifice of Christ, opening up a new and living way for us — the way to life — gives us confidence, a full assurance, a clean conscience.

We each demonstrate that fresh, clean conscience by being baptized. That's what he's referring to in that last phrase of 10:22, "our bodies washed with pure water." Baptism is a corporate endorsement of someone's salvation. It's not just you, as an individual, making a statement, "I've been washed in the blood. I have a clean conscience and so I can come to God now." It is that but it is also the church saying, "We believe you have been washed in the blood; that you have a clean conscience and so you can come to God now."

So, since we can draw near to God, we should. Since we can come together to the Father, we should. We should want to. "Better is one day in your house than thousands elsewhere!" (Ps. 84 :10). The house now is not a temple in the Middle East or a building we call a "church" but the presence of God with the gathered family of

God. So now we can draw near to God. Since we can, we should. Then, since we're drawing nearer to God, we are to draw near to each other; that if I belong to Christ then I belong to the Body of Christ. If I belong to God, I belong to the house of God.

Holding & Considering Together

The second thing we are to do on the common foundation we have of Christ's blood, is to "hold fast the confession of our hope without wavering" (Heb. 10:23). That is, we are to continue to believe in the eternal life, the access to the Father, the forgiveness of sins bought for us by the blood of Christ. We continue to confess that great salvation because, "He who promised is faithful." So, if God is faithful, holding onto us, then we can hold onto the promise of salvation without waffling. Continue to believe in what Jesus did for you without feeling the urge to believe in what you can do for him, like religious rituals. Don't start to put part of your faith in a church, even one that claims it is the true church, that believing in it is the same as believing in Jesus. The true church is a "pillar and buttress of the truth" (1 Tim. 3:15). That is, it holds up the truth, not its own reputation. Beware of a church that is constantly telling you to believe in it; that believing in it is the same as believing in Jesus. We have one hope that we are, as a church, to hold on to and hold up together.

Finally, we are to consider together. We are told, "And let us consider how to stir up one another to love and good works" (Heb. 10:24). Who are you supposed to consider? In other words, who is the "one another"? The key question — who do you belong to? — is not whether we believe in attending church, any church. It's who you belong to, which body of people. The issue of church membership is not what organized, religious corporation you will attend and give to, not what building will you go to, but what group of other believers you will be committed to. Who is the "one another" that we're supposed to consider?

If you take the individualistic, church-as-restaurant view to its logical conclusion, the church is for me being "fed," for me getting my blessing. Or it's like a gas station; it's an inspiration station where I go to get my spiritual tank filled up. Or a theater; it's where I go for the biblical show. If you take these models of the church to their logical conclusion, they will destroy the church. People will drift from church to church, depending on which is catering to their needs as a religious consumer. Or maybe they'll stay but they won't be committed to the people; they're committed to an organization or a building. Or maybe they'll decide to stay home and watch their favorite celebrity pastor on TV or the internet. They know who they belong to and it isn't the church, the people, the other members, the Body of Christ.

The key question is whether you should belong to a specific church, be committed to particular fellow-believers, covenanted to one local church. Hebrews 10:24 answers that question. Consider how to stir up one another. What "one another"? That is, which specific people, exactly, are you are supposed to be considering? If you don't know that, you can't obey that passage. Who are you called on to ponder? You are instructed to think about what you can do for some particular people. Who? That's what membership answers. Your fellow members are the ones you are commanded to consider. If you only consider those you feel like considering at any given time, you'll be like that lady who piously mouths, "I know who I belong to," talking about her "church family" as she drifts from church to church. But for you to keep the call to consider one another, the "one another" must be a specific group of people, names you know, faces you can see.

Church Discipline & the Body

We see this over and over again in the New Testament. How can you obey the Lord Jesus' command in Matthew 18:15–18 — if you see your brother in sin, go, then bring others, then, if necessary, tell it to the church — without committed membership in a particular church? How do you know someone is a brother? How do you know that they are in sin? (It implies involvement in others' lives.) Who do you inform when someone continues in sin? If you can put someone outside, doesn't that mean that there is an inside? Membership defines who is inside. Matthew 18:15–18 is the only passage where the Lord Jesus specifically mentions the "church" and instructs it what to do. It is impossible to obey him without church membership.

Jesus's one specific instruction to the local church destroys the church-as-theater mentality. He could have given us detailed by-laws on how he wants his churches organized. He didn't. Instead, he gave them one explicit direction on what they must do. He addresses Matthew 18:15–18 to us, his followers. This is what we must do if we're truly following Jesus. You must know who your brother or sister is, know who you can bring to intervene, know who you can bring the matter before and who exactly are the body of people someone can be put out of, if necessary. Jesus said, "if he [or she] refuses to listen even to the assembly," then he or she should be removed from that assembly. So, he or she and you must first be a part of that assembly, the church. If you're not in a relationship with a church where you can follow those instructions, you are out of the will of God.

What Jesus shows us in Matthew 18:15 is pregnant with volumes of plans for church membership. He tells us we are to accurately know who is our spiritual family members — who we're responsible to approach. In Jesus' plan for the church, the church helps you gain your brother or sister. If the church is just a concert hall for the performance of your favorite preachers or musicians, then it doesn't matter how you feel about the back of the head you see in front of you. They're just objects you hope don't block your view when the show starts. But in Jesus' plan for the church, they are members of the body to which you are attached.

Four consecutive chapters in 1 Corinthians are impossible to understand without believing in church membership. In 1 Corinthians 11, we're first told that women should have a sign of authority if they're to "pray or prophesy" in the church. Whose authority does the sign point to? Then, we're told to "discern the Body" before taking the Lord's Supper (1 Cor. 11:29). That means contemplate the other members of the Body, about your impact on them. Consider your fellow members before taking the Lord's Supper. Without membership, how do you know who to discern? 1 Corinthians 12 says that we are, together, one body with many members, that each member has different gifts. If you're not a committed part of a local church, how are you contributing your gifts to the body? What body? Do you even know which body your gifts are supposed to be a part of? Do you help other members use their gifts? How can you be a detached, uncommitted member, like an arm, going from body to body?

1 Corinthians 13, the great "love chapter," is about relationships in the body. If you're not committed to a specific church, who are you being patient with; who are you being kind with; who are you not envying; who, exactly, are you being not boasting to; who are you not being angered by; whose wrongs are you not keeping a record of; who are you protecting, trusting, hoping for, persevering for, never failing? Who exactly? If a member bears, believes, hopes and endures all things (of other members), will he or she leave for a frivolous reason? To be entertained somewhere else? Then in the next chapter, 1 Corinthians 14, we're told to bring our gifts for the building up of the church, an actual, specific church. Who are you building up?

God's Idea of the Church

In Hebrews 10:24 we are commanded to think — a special kind of thinking, think together, to get together and plot and scheme, form plans, not against each other but conspire to help each other love and do good works. We're called to form little conspiracies of kindness, "how can we get that John to be more loving and do more good things?" Maybe we see a member with a need. Maybe they seem a little down. Their family is not helpful. Look especially after members who don't have other family as members. Allow some groups to develop, groups of friends, form disciplining relationships, to small groups that meet together for prayer, perhaps just meet to talk, to eat together, get to know each other so you can know precisely how to encourage them. Build networks across different kinds of people, so that cliques of the same kinds of people don't become exclusive. Encourage the young to relate to the old, the white to the black to the Asian, the married to the single. This is God's idea of the church: a conspiracy of kindness, intent on helping each other love and give. But you have to know who to "stir up," to provoke, to incite to love and good works. Who, exactly, are you called on to conspire to be kind to? Who do you belong to? No, it's not just Christ, by himself without his Body.

Who do you belong to? If you don't know exactly who, if you can't say, "I know who I belong to" and see specific people — name names, see faces — you'll drift to whoever is convenient; whoever does the most for you, like a shopper looking for weekly specials. Hebrews 10:24 suggests that loving one another will not just happen. It needs to be worked at, even provoked. It requires huddles and consulting. While we still can, all of us are to get together and plan how can we help each other be more loving and generous and do it more and more, as the day of Jesus' return nears.

Church membership, then, is not just like going to a restaurant where your only consideration is whether you are getting what you want. Is the food good, the service friendly and prompt, the place clean, the ambiance attractive? That is the individualism of consumerism. The acids of that attitude dissolve the church. In God's idea of the church, we come together to consider — not first what are we getting out of it — but what can we do to help another believer grow; what can I do for this particular body? How can we, working together, create a house of God where those we are attached to become more loving and do more and more good works? That's the church.

To do that, one thing is absolutely necessary: we have to attend. The church is a body with many parts. We can all be doing different things. Allowing for different members to use their gifts is a pillar of a biblical church. We can't expect everyone else to be gifted to do the things we are gifted to do. We're one body with many members, members doing different things. But there is one thing that all who are able absolutely must do: we must attend. The command in Hebrews 10:25 applies to all Christians; all who are physically able to attend, are told to do so. That's the only way you can join in the holy conspiracies, follow Jesus' plan for discipline, discern the body, use your gift in the body, and bear, believe, hope and endure all things when you are tempted to go for the show somewhere else.

We see that in the meaning of the word "church." It is the *ekklesia*, which simply means "assembly" or "gathering." If someone is not assembling, how can they possibly be part of the assembly? To put it succinctly, except in the case of shut-ins and the like, if he is not regularly assembling, he shouldn't be a church member.

Church membership, then, is a covenant commitment, like a marriage. In a marriage, the wedding vows define that covenant commitment: the commitment means I will love, honor and cherish, forsaking all others, until death do us part. "I know who I belong to": you. For our church, that commitment is defined by our church covenant, which is a summation of the commitments scripture tells us to make. We are saying we belong to each other, to walk together in Christian love. Our love for other members is shown in specific ways, spelled out in scripture, reflected in our covenant. Just as the membership roll tells us exactly who we are to be considering, the covenant tells us exactly how we're to be considering, what "love and good works" we're to be conspiring to provoke.

For example, the covenant, echoing the Bible, tells us to give. Members commit to support the church financially, share with the assembly. The member who comes, devours the worship, the preaching, the fellowship and then doesn't give is not a bad customer, akin to a restaurant customer who leaves before paying his bill. He's someone who's not considering others. The tie between giving and fellowship is so great, it's difficult to tell, sometimes, when a New Testament word for fellowship refers to a communion of spiritual siblings or to a monetary gift. The key word is "*koinonia*," translated in Acts 2:42 as "the fellowship," and in 2 Corinthians 9:13 as "contribution." When the Corinthians give, the poor Christians in Jerusalem will, Paul says, "long for them," they'll be attached, relationally, and they will pray for them. We give to promote fellowship. Commitment is spelled: M-O-N-E-Y. Having made that commitment everything changes. We realize we can't shrug each other off and say, "I know who I belong to" (and it's not you). If we belong to Christ, we belong to his Body. That's not just theoretical, like claiming to believe in the universal church while refusing to commit to a specific church. That's like a man refusing to commit to one, specific woman because, he says, he believes in the "universal woman." No, as much as our culture instills in us that consumer-mentality, that this and every relationship, exist for my customer satisfaction and if it doesn't deliver, I'll drift off to the next one, whether church or spouse; as much as we're tempted to slip right back into our individualistic, self-centered consumerism in which the only thing we plot to do is to have it our way, we need, finally, to be converted in our minds, to look at other members of the church and ask "What can I do to help them?"

So, we're committed not just to our own customer-satisfaction but to each other. To specific people. To names we know. To faces we can see. "Church membership" — the pillar of a biblical church — is not another word for church attendance; that as long as you're attending somewhere, in a church building, it's okay; that it doesn't matter which one, specifically, you're going to, like a man thinking it doesn't matter which woman, specifically, he's with; whether his wife or someone else; just as long as he's with a woman. No. In marriage we ask that a man to be committed to a specific woman. In church membership, we ask you to be committed to a specific church, specific names and faces.

PILLAR SIX

Leadership & Followership

1 Timothy 5:17–19, 2 Timothy 4:1–2,
Titus 2:15, Hebrews 13:17

DOES "PSEUDOCYESIS" RING A BELL? In chapter two, "God according to God," I described pseudocyesis. It is false pregnancy, the condition of thinking that you are expecting a baby when you really are not. Women with pseudocyesis have many, if not all, the symptoms of pregnancy, even the distended abdomen — but no actual baby. The psyche isn't able to produce one of those. They so want a child that their mind fools their body that they have one until it comes time to deliver and there's no baby. I guess many (probably most) women with that condition in developed countries eventually accept what pregnancy tests and ultra-sounds show is the truth. So they don't have to wait until they aren't able to give birth. Unless, of course, they purposely avoid those tests, not wanting to know the truth.

I became aware of this condition about a decade ago when a member of our church repeatedly thought she was pregnant when she wasn't. When one of our mature women informally counseled her, the mature lady told me that the other member (probably with pseudocyesis) had a lot of psychological issues. She left us soon after, of course. I say, "of course," because I've found on several occasions that it is the people with the most problems — spiritual or psychological — who don't want their problems exposed or dealt with. On several occasions when it became clear that a person needs some kind of professional counseling, it is exactly at that moment that they leave.

Once, a young man was so hysterical that I suggested we pay for his counseling. Instead, he left amid a flurry of false accusations and is now the "pastor of discipleship" at a mega church. Another man showed himself to be so duplicitous — his actual life was so different than his words — that I recommended that he see a counselor who specialized in "reality therapy." Reality therapy means making the patient deal with reality. Reality therapy would challenge the duplicitous member about the disparity between what he said and how he really lived.

Perhaps one of the biggest differences between treating people with physical health needs — medicine — and people with psychological and spiritual health needs, is that the psychologically and spiritually sick often don't want help. Indeed, one of the symptoms of some psychological or spiritual diseases is not wanting it dealt with; not wanting it exposed by diagnosis; not wanting it treated. Most people, as soon as they get physically sick, want it treated and cured but people with spiritual problems often run from treatment. They will especially dislike someone with authority who will speak the truth to them.

The psychiatrist M. Scott Peck wrote an interesting book entitled *People of the Lie.* In it, he notes this very dynamic: that often the neediest, the evil people, the most malicious and troubled, rarely seek professional help. He writes,

> Since they will do almost anything to avoid the particular pain that comes from self-examination, under ordinary circumstances the evil are the last people who would ever come to psychotherapy. The evil hate the light — the light of goodness that shows them up, the light of scrutiny that exposes them, the light of truth that penetrates their deception.

He says that such people are masters of disguise, of covering up their needs, their sins, the reality of who they are. But, if they would rather do anything than be where they could be exposed, Dr. Peck says that they are often attracted to a place where now, their disguise will remain intact: the church. In a footnote, probably a much over-looked passage, he writes,

> Since the primary motive of the evil is disguise, one of the places where evil people are most likely to be found is within the church. What better way to conceal one's evil from oneself, as well as from others, than to be a deacon or some other highly visible form of Christian within our culture. . . . Evil people tend to gravitate toward piety for the disguise and concealment it can offer them. (p. 76.)

Of course, that assumes that the church is a good place to hide one's sin; that the Word won't be applied to them; that the leadership won't be allowed to challenge them; that the leaders can be intimidated, bullied, bribed or flattered into not preaching the Word to them, particularly applying it to their needs; that the church, especially the leadership, will enable them to stay in their sin; that they'll be comforted in it, rather than reproved, rebuked and exhorted with all authority. That assumption is right, most of the time, because of the way, often, churches are in our culture. But one of the pillars of a biblical church is that it is not like that; that the pastor, the elders, preach the Word to the needs of the people; that the light shines into the darkness.

What does a "pastor" do? Four key passages tell us. Each of them, in their own way, say he (or they) labor in preaching and teaching, preach the Word, they correct the people with the Word; they are listened to. They don't just give lectures on abstract Bible knowledge detached from the life of the people in front of them. They apply it to them, even to change them. They don't only comfort the afflicted; they sometimes afflict the comfortable. That's why the only place in the Bible where the noun "pastor" occurs, in Ephesians 4:11, it is connected with "teacher." He teaches, not just to give information but to pastor, to shepherd, to lead people in the right way. He speaks the truth in love for the specific purpose of the Body growing up.

1 Timothy 5:17-19

The men we normally call "pastors" are called "elders" who "labor in preaching and teaching." He begins, "Let the elders" — plural (that's the model, not the command) — who rule well be honored. "Rule" or "direct" shows that the elders are leading the church. Those who rule well should be "considered worthy of a double honor," more honor, apparently than the other elders. They all deserve honor or else they shouldn't be elders. Then, especially, among those who rule well, another smaller group within the body of the elders, are those who "labor in preaching and teaching."

The word for "labor" means to toil, to work hard, strenuous work that results in weariness and fatigue. Almost every Sunday evening, after the preaching is done and I'm home lying on the couch, I'm overcome by a weight of fatigue. Monday is my day to recover from that weariness. This is not the kind of work one can do on the side, as a hobby, merely after completing one's secular employment for the week. "Labor" suggests that it was full-time work.

The next verse, 1 Timothy 5:18, shows that they are paid. "You shall not muzzle an ox when it treads out the grain," quoting the Deuteronomy 25:4; and "The laborer deserves his wages," quoting Jesus. The idea that the paid ministry was a later corruption of the church is wrong. Singapore introduced me to the Plymouth Brethren churches which tried to reproduce a vision of churches with no professional ministry, only lay-elders. I found no greater advertisement for the need for seminary training than the attempts at preaching I heard from well-meaning but ungifted and unprepared elders. The Plymouth Brethren vision of the New Testament church was an illusion. Biblical churches financially support their pastors. While all members of the church are priests, some are particularly gifted in preaching and teaching. Their gifting for those tasks demonstrates, among other things, their calling to work in preaching and teaching. The church should cultivate those members who have those special gifts and then, when mature, financially support them. They should also expect that these paid pastors support the church with their generous giving as much as, if not more, than any other member of the church. Indeed, a man who will make his living off of the voluntary offerings of Christian people who does not also contribute to the church is probably not fit for the ministry. It's monumental hypocrisy to weekly stand before members one is asking to give and not, oneself, give generously.

What's he doing, though, with this "laboring in preaching and teaching"? Is it just educating? No. Is it just confirming people in what they already believe? It's not supposed to be but how did we get into a situation where today a leading psychiatrist could note that evil people gravitate to the church because it's the best environment to hide their sin in? Once someone told me that I should not preach something that someone in the church might not agree with. I guess I should ask the members to write down for me all the things they currently believe, maybe list the "sins" (they may not agree are sins) they want to cling to, so I know what subjects I'm supposed to steer clear from, because preaching, is about confirming us as we already are. It's enabling, so that person thought.

The opposite of a leader (for the church) is not a follower. We need followers. Good followers empower good leaders. The opposite of a leader is an enabler. For the church, a leader challenges people with the Word of God, exposes their sin, rebukes if necessary, leads them to repentance, to change. A biblical leader helps people follow Christ. An enabler helps people stay comfortable in their sins, to stay as they are, unexposed, unchallenged, unconfronted. An enabling parent helps his or her kids be comfortable, no matter what their decisions. When, several years ago, our son's high school football team stormed the field, outraged at the other team, and the game was forfeited because of that, some of the parents of the ruffians got on Facebook complaining about the referees canceling the game. It's the referees' fault, they wailed. I thought, "your boys are undisciplined ruffians because you are enablers; instead of holding them responsible, you're excusing them." That's why one of the most offensive things you can do to people who want to be enabled is to try to lead them to repentance; to shine the light of the Word on their sin, on their heart. They will cringe and scream and bitterly complain that you're not a good leader (or mother or father or coach), because they want an enabler.

Enablers (or people who crave them) reflexively blame the leader. That's why we're told in 1 Timothy 5:19, "Do not admit a charge against an elder except on the evidence of two or three witnesses." Do not "admit" or receive or entertain, in other words, give it no weight; don't consider it, certainly don't jump to the conclusion that it's true. Don't accept an accusation against an elder (and a pastor is an elder) unless there are two or three witnesses to corroborate it. John Calvin commented on this passage:

> This [protection from uncorroborated accusations] is not merely owing to the higher degree of moral excellence which is demanded from them, but because almost all are tempted by Satan to excessive credulity, so that, without making any inquiry, they eagerly condemn their pastors, whose good name they ought rather to have defended. (Commentary on 1 Timothy 5:19.)

This is an almost unimaginable instruction in today's American evangelical church.

Pastors having to endure false accusations is now par for the course, among large swaths of the church culture. One piece of advice I heard was that when a pastor is falsely accused, just admit to the charge, apologize and start sending résumés out to other churches so you can get a new position before the next wave of false accusations comes crashing down. Once, I got a letter full of false accusations, including that I had put a kid in a "head-lock," based on something the accuser had heard, second-hand, exactly the kind of accusation that 1 Timothy 5:19 tells us not to even entertain. In response, I detailed point by point the facts in a reply letter. Despite most of the accusations being debunked, the false accuser never apologized, as though repeating second hand charges and jumping to conclusions is okay if it's done against a pastor. Someone else said I should just live with it, like it's part of the job description. The Word of God says it should never happen in the church.

What would happen to a sports team if the players could vote on the coach? Would they start to grumble and threaten to fire him if he started working them out too hard — what they thought was too hard? Would they fire him if he made changes they didn't like? In the church, we have to have the congregations' approval. (You can vote with your feet, by leaving, and there's nothing we can do about that.) But that means you need the maturity to go along with things that are uncomfortable, to be supportive, even when you don't always agree, as long as they're not unbiblical, of course. We need church members who are mature enough to not grumble. We need members who take 1 Timothy 5:19 seriously and so don't encourage unfounded criticism or reflexively blame the pastor. You need to know that you need leadership, that a pillar of a biblical church is allowing the leaders to do what leaders are supposed to do. You need to learn the art of followership.

They say when a culture values or experiences something a lot, it has many words for it. Eskimos have fifty words for snow, for the different kinds of snow that they live with. But we have no word for the art of following. We have "leadership" for the art of leading but no proper word for the art of following, what would logically be "followership." We have no such word. Type it into a computer and it will put red dashes under it; auto-correct will divide it into two words: follow and ship. That's because we don't respect following. But leaders need followers.

2 Timothy 4:1-2

What's the pastor supposed to do? Paul is writing to Timothy, the "pastor." Paul begins 2 Timothy 4, extremely seriously, calling God the Father and the Lord Jesus Christ, the One who will be the Judge of all people who ever lived, to witness this. Pay attention Timothy. Pay attention modern church member. John Calvin preached,

"The man who is not shaken out of his carelessness and laziness by the thought that the government of the church is conducted under the eye of God and his angels must be worse than stupid, and have a heart harder than stone" (Calvin's commentary on 1 Timothy 5:21.) The pastor is charged: proclaim the Word. He's not charged with doing hours of home visitation or to visit the hospital every day or to spend his time in counseling or socializing. He's called to proclaim the Word. Be ready to do it, he says, "in season and out of season." In good times and bad times. Do it when the church is growing and people are excited and everything is new and even Wednesday nights are overflowing. Do it in bad times when people are distracted and discouraged and the church seems to be dwindling.

We probably understand that: endurance, keep going even when it's hard. Here's where it starts to get strange, in this culture where the church is a haven for evil people because they know that their sin won't be exposed there; where pastors are told to be enablers.

"Preach the word." But what's he doing with the Word? Is it a theological lecture? Is he telling us about all the verb tenses and participles and conditional clauses so we go away with an excellent understanding of the grammar of this verse and next week, we'll hear the next verse taken apart word by word? Maybe that's how it starts. But that's not all. Notice, next, 2 Timothy 4:2, three things: reprove, rebuke, and exhort.

To "reprove" is to correct. Don't try to serve God and money; you can't do it. Don't have sex outside of marriage. Implied is that it is his people who are being reproved, corrected, not the pagan people in Rome, not the uncouth barbarians; not the liberals in Hollywood or the Mormons in Utah. Reprove the people in the church. Make the Word relevant to their lives.

Then, "rebuke." Rebuke you! It's the opposite of enabling. To "rebuke" is a sharper form of correction: stop doing that; repent of making an idol out of wealth; repent of your fornication, of watching pornography, stoking lust; repent of enabling sin. "Stop it."

"Exhort" is more positive and encouraging; it's to come alongside someone to help them do it the right way and it's probably the one of the three things a pastor does with preaching the Word that we understand: let me show you how to raise your kids better, to not enable their sin; seek first the Kingdom of God, to live a life of purity. Again, all these things — reprove, rebuke, exhort — are taking the Word and applying to the people in the church. Why would a pastor do that? Because of what the church is. In 1 Timothy, it's a gymnasium of godliness, where you go to be trained to be more like God, in your character. When I was running track, one workout the coach tells us to run such-and-such a distance and I take off, thinking the best way to start, to accelerate, is by "over-striding," stretching my stride length. The coach stopped us, called us together and gave a brief little lesson, reproving, on not over-striding. He was talking specifically about me but he thought while he was correcting me, he might as well correct the whole team. I was glad for the instruction because I wanted to be a better runner. You should be glad for correction at church because you want to be a better Christian. So, if you feel like someday your pastor is talking directly to you — reproving, rebuking, or exhorting — your reaction should be, "Thank you!"

Now, the pastor is to do these three things "with complete patience and teaching." The "patience" is not only the tone, a gentle tone, usually; but also that he patiently keeps doing it, with "long-suffering," often suffering through other people's failures to understand. You continue teaching. You don't give up because you think, "I've been teaching these people for 12 years and it hasn't made any difference." You teach them with doctrine: show that the covetousness is idolatry; that the Kingdom of God is the great treasure and so if you must close your shop on Sunday morning and make less money, that's a sacrifice you must make; that the husband is the head of the wife like Christ is the head of the church so to give up that headship in the home just to have peace is like a church compromising the headship of Christ just to make some trouble-makers happy; show them that your body is a temple of the Holy Spirit and so you can't engage it in sexual immorality. The pastor reproves, rebukes — corrects sharply, sometimes — and exhorts, encourages, inspires you to do better, to have a vision of the great truths that fill you with hope that propel you forward, that puts wind in your sails, each of these three things, patiently, consistently.

Now, in our culture where kids are raised on being told how great they are, where Christian radio stations sell themselves on being exclusively "positive and encouraging" — just the exhorting, not the reproving and rebuking — where churches are often havens for evil people, where church members seriously tell their pastor that he shouldn't preach anything that someone in the church might disagree with, where enablers are wanted — what do you think the chances are that some people are going to be offended by a pastor who doesn't just exhort but also reproves and rebukes? There will be offended people, maybe some trying to hide who they really are, trying to hide from the Word and they will want to disregard the ministry of the Word. They'll despise it; stifle it; ignore it. That's how we got to this condition that even some churches are havens for evil people, isn't it? The ministry of the Word can be made irrelevant, an exercise in enabling. How did the church grow in the South for over a century side-by-side with racism without a lot of enabling? Racism and church growth could only co-exist if the church was dysfunctional, if pastors were enabling. Even if racism has partly waned, are we now enabling other sins?

Titus 2:15

What are we to do? "Declare these things; exhort and rebuke with all authority. Let no one disregard you." Paul addresses Titus, the "pastor" (an elder) of the church in Cyprus. In this passage we zero in on what church leadership is about. What exactly does a spiritual leader do? Is he an enabler who helps people feel comfortable as they are? Is he an orator trying to evoke a feeling in you? Is he a therapist who feels your pain? Is he a manager who coordinates programs and people for the purpose of numerical growth? Is he a master of ceremonies, an inoffensive icon who looks and sounds winsome, like a game-show host? Is he a guardian of conventional morality and the old-time religion?

First, notice Paul tells Titus to "declare these things." "Declare" is an authoritative word. He didn't say "suggest" these things, imply them, hint at them, nag about them. Declare. These things are the things he instructed to various groups of people in the church: older men, older women, younger women and younger men. The older women, by the way, can teach the younger women, and so we see that some of the ministry can be delegated. The pastor does not have to do it all. He is to speak these things and exhort and "rebuke" or "reprove," again.

Then, how are spiritual leaders to declare, exhort and rebuke? Apologetically? Timidly? No. "With all authority," literally "by command." In other words, speak it — all the instructions above to the people, encouraging, sure, but also correcting — with a command, not a suggestion; with authority because you, Titus, pastor, have authority. Here's the kicker, probably the most interesting command in all of scripture, to the pastor, "Let no one disregard you."

How do you not "let anyone disregard you"? That is, do not allow yourself, Titus, pastor, to be ignored, to be looked down on, to be considered the punching bag who can be blamed for everything, who has to take every accusation (from the members) because we Americans believe — shaped by a culture where we legally can say anything we want about our political leaders —the pastor can be accused of anything? Don't take being disregarded, disrespected. What a strange command! Do not tolerate being ignored, treated disrespectfully, falsely accused, blamed reflexively.

Hebrews 13:17

What does followship look like? "Obey your leaders and submit to them, for they are keeping watch over your souls, as those who will have to give an account. Let them do this with joy and not with groaning, for that would be of no advantage to you." Hebrews

13:17 is probably the most unpopular verse in the Bible; more unpopular to modern, American Christians than that one in the psalms about dashing infants against rocks (Ps. 137:9). The writer uses one of the most offensive words to Americans today. The "S" word: submit. "Obey your leaders and submit to them." Think how strange that sounds to our ears, especially in a culture in which authority figures are doubted from the get-go. "Obey," "submit," to leaders.

The reflex of the modern American is to immediately recoil in horror, exclaiming warnings about the dangers of "pastoral abuse." There is a danger of abuse. Pastors are sinners and have the potential to use authority to feed their flesh. Ideally, one of the checks on that potential for abuse is that a church has multiple elders. "Leaders" is plural in Hebrews 13:17. But that's not always possible as the numbers of men gifted and qualified to be elders is not large. Congregationalism — that the members have a say in the direction of the church — is also a check. If necessary, they can dismiss an abusive pastor and even excommunicate him. But if our reflex is to assume that the church exists to oversee the pastor, we've lost sight of what the church is for. By his maturity and self-control, the pastor should be the member of the church who least needs accountability. His calling is to provide accountability to others, normally through his preaching. There is a problem of abuse in American churches. But in my opinion the most common form of abuse is over-bearing, sometimes fraudulent, members abusing their pastors.

Because I spent the first half of my adult life as a regular church member, attending church, listening to sermons and Sunday School lessons, I was surprised to find, when I became a pastor, that there is a kind of person who treated me worse for it. Once, we handed out a sign-up sheet for slots to work for a church project and someone commented, to the entire congregation, that I hadn't signed up. (I was going to wait until everyone else signed up and then fill in the empty slots myself.) The man who spoke up presumptuously would never think of singling out for embarrassment anyone else in the congregation: only the pastor. This instinct to esteem the pastor least seems to be a problem of one particular culture, namely mine. I have a joke, based on real life: In the Chinese church, they call the pastor's wife, "Mrs. Pastor." In the Black church, they call the pastor's wife, "First Lady." In the white church, they call the pastor's wife to tell her the bathroom is dirty.

There is a kind of person who assumes that he or she knows better than the pastor does about anything, about how to have a prayer meeting, how to pray publicly, how to preach, how to visit. I once had a woman absolutely berate me, in front of others, for the way I was leading the Wednesday night prayer meeting. I was thinking, "You wouldn't think of treating the average person like this but only because I'm a pastor and I'm supposed to be especially patient, you think you can get away with being so rude."

Hebrews 13:17 says we are to "Obey our leaders — maybe it could be, "be confident in them" — and submit to them." Don't resist them for no reason. Then it gives a reason to follow: "for they are keeping watch over your souls." Leaders have a responsibility, before God, to monitor your spiritual condition. That's part of what membership means: it means you have committed to be watched and led by your pastors and for the pastors it means they have a responsibility to watch over their members. Your life is their business. I will have to answer to God for my members. When it comes time for me to give account of my ministry and God asks me why I let so-and-so slip into a destructive relationship, or some sin, why I enabled someone to feel good about doing bad, it's not going to be a very good answer if the only thing I can say is, "I was afraid they wouldn't like me anymore"! The spiritual leader is called to be popular, in the end, with only one person.

Notice who your leaders are. They are those who are keeping (present tense, right now) watch over your soul. They're monitoring you. They aren't just some guy on the radio or internet you like to listen to. They're not your favorite celebrity pastor. It's great if you get extra encouragement from faithful people outside your local church but those are not your leaders. They are no more your leaders than the chef behind the counter at your favorite restaurant is your wife (or husband). Your leaders are those who are keeping watch — a long-term, continuous relationship; people you belong to and they belong to you. They know you and so can apply the Word specifically to you. They'll have to answer to God for how they watched over your soul. So, let them do this with joy; because you're someone who listens, someone who wants to grow and wants to hear the Word even if it exposes your sin and calls you to repentance. Don't let them have to do it with groaning, "Ugh, again, for the thousandth time I have to tell him (or her) not to love money." "I'm being accused again." "He's not listening to me; what's the use?!" Don't do that because that makes church dreary.

Plurality of Elders

The one feature of biblical church leadership that has become popular today is the "plurality of eldership." It's a clumsy way of saying have more than one elder in a church. That's a fine ideal. The churches mentioned in the New Testament had multiple elders. Of course, they also included all Christians in a given area, unlike we who have many churches operating side-by-side in the same area. Probably every area in the USA, then, has multiple elders, even if the particular local churches do not. Nevertheless, beware of the prima donna who wants to be the sole man at the top. That the Biblical example is multiple elders means that we should seek to have them if we can. However, the Bible doesn't actually command churches to have multiple elders. It commands them to sing psalms but not have more than one elder. It models it for us but doesn't tell us to do it.

This leads to the can-of-worms question as to when are the indicatives in Acts and the epistles imperatives or when are they just history? Those who argue that we should have the Lord's Supper every Sunday point to passages, especially Acts 2:42, that show the Apostolic church was dedicated to the "breaking of bread" (which they assume is the Lord's Supper) and then further assume that we have to follow their example; that their indicative is our imperative. First, "breaking bread" is not a code word for the Lord's Supper or else the Lord Jesus was serving the Lord's Supper to the two disciples on the road to Emmaus (Luke 24:30) and the Apostle Paul was serving it to the pagan sailors adrift in the Mediterranean Sea (Acts 27:35). Second, there isn't one command in the Bible for the church to have the Lord's Supper every Lord's Day, just as there is no command for a church to have multiple elders.

Willy-nilly advising churches to have multiple elders, without knowing if they have qualified men in their membership, is as unwise as telling a young man to marry one of the single women he currently knows. Maybe none of them are fit to be his wife. Maybe a church simply doesn't have men who are both gifted and mature enough to be elders. Making one of them into an elder just to fill a quota can lead to disaster. This is especially so in our modern, consumeristic culture. The modern self Carl Truman describes bends institutions, like the church, to become "servants of the individual." So they "cease to be places for the formation of individuals. . . . They become platforms for performance. . . . Churches are places where one goes to perform, not be formed" (*The Rise and Triumph of the Modern Self*, p. 49.) That is, churches become a venue to flaunt one's religiosity. This is especially the case in the rural South, where, I believe, many men seek to be the big man in church. I joke that half the men in my county think that they are preachers. Few of them are willing to invest the time and hard work into the calling.

There aren't as many qualified men to be elders as some of those advising us to have a "plurality of elders" imagine. If your church has men who aren't disqualified, according to 1 Timothy 3:1–7 and Titus 1:7–8, and who are qualified to hold fast to the Word, instruct in sound doctrine and rebuke those who contradict it (Titus 1:9); if they are true pastors, even if they're not preaching regularly, then, by all means, make them elders. But elders aren't a board of directors. They are pastors. Multiple elders, if a church can have them, are a team of pastors. They should share the pastoral care of the members. Of the pastors I've sat under, most were good at pastoral care. When my father died, when I was 21, my pastor, who had been visiting my father as his cancer progressed, came to the funeral, even though my father was not a member of his church. But no lay-elder did. I had an elder who was supposed to be responsible for me. He didn't come. Indeed, I have no recollection of him communicating condolences to me in any way. As a pastor, I've had elders who think their role is to convey to me the needs for pastoral care that I should take care of, without doing it themselves. In the push for a "plurality of elders," such experiences are likely common.

The man who desires to be an elder desires a noble task (1 Tim. 3:1) but he doesn't always desire it for noble reasons. In modern American culture, if a man hasn't been transformed by the Word, if he thinks like the secular culture around him, such a man thrust into leadership will see himself as the inspector general of the church, empowered above all to be the pastor's critic, a check on the pastor, the Republican to the pastor's Democrat, yearning for spot-light time while not necessarily bound to the members with that blessed tie. If he doesn't get his title and up-front time, he'll leave the members to go find a platform for performance elsewhere. Or he may think he's the church's quality control. In a consumer culture, a plurality of elders may see themselves not as a team of pastors to share the pastoral care but as quality control for the product the church is putting out. The customer is still king, the worldly elder thinks, and so if the customer is not satisfied, the plural elders will file the complaint. Or he may try to be both: a political check on the pastor and quality control but little pastoral care of the members. Ecclesiological gurus glibly advising us of the benefits of a "plurality of elders," as though capable, qualified, biblically-transformed leaders are just lying around waiting to be picked up are as helpful as Marie Antoinette advising poor, breadless peasants to eat cake.

Who Are Your Leaders?

Your spiritual leaders are those who are keeping watch over your soul, who are telling you the truth, even if, sometimes, you don't want to hear it, who will give you some "reality therapy" with the

Word of God. You listen to them because you believe God has given them authority for you.

I believe pastoral authority is the key to understand another hot issue today: the role of women in ministry. When we water down Hebrews 13:17 (and other such passages) to mean nothing, as some do, then there are no people in the church we should especially listen to; there's no authority. There's just speakers or non-speakers. Your church leaders, you think, have no more authority in your life than a professor at college; maybe less, since the pastor can't even grade you. Or, they have no more authority than an actor on a stage. So when you come to 1 Corinthians 11:2–16 that tells us that women can speak in church (but should do so with a sign of authority) and 1 Timothy 2:12 that says women can't be in authority over men, you have to choose between two errors: either women can't speak at all because we confuse speaking with having authority or that women can speak just like men and so we can have women pastors and elders. But not all speakers are leaders. Some who speak in church are under authority and others are in authority and we should heed them. The leaders are the speakers who have authority in my life. Others, maybe women, can speak but do not have authority over my life. They are under authority; that's why in their culture, they wore a head covering; under authority they could "pray and prophesy" (1 Cor. 11:3). There's so much confusion on this issue in our culture because we don't understand authority. Men, as elders, have authority. Women can't be elders or in authority but they can speak and minister. People don't understand the role of women in ministry because they don't understand the role of men in ministry.

Your leaders are people who know you and apply the Word of God to your life. In larger churches, not every leader, like the senior pastor, can know you intimately, but there are other elders who will. Together, corporately, the eldership knows you. So, virtual church — "virtch" — is impossible. First, "church" means assembly, not spectating. We can watch a church on-line or on TV but we can't be part of one that way. Second, salient here, the leaders can't get to know you very well on-line. Even if the communication is two-way, your revealing yourself will be selective, edited, filtered through the medium. Leaders may use technology to supplement their communication but it shouldn't be their main medium. Why else have pastors if they aren't going to apply the Word directly to us? Why not have actors dramatize C. H. Spurgeon sermons or have a VJ cue up the best sermon videos of preaching super-stars around the world? We might learn a lot about the Bible that way. We might be inspired. Of course, our particular needs will never be dealt with.

God's design is that churches have pastors. Pastors are imperfect men, sinners like anyone else. But it is through them that the Word of God is preached, taught, applied, sometimes, even used to rebuke, correct, expose our embarrassing sins that we are tempted to hide.

PILLAR 7

God-centered Worship

Hebrews 12:28–29, Colossians 3:16

I ARRIVED IN PASADENA, CALIFORNIA, from Alabama, in mid-
September of 1987 to start seminary. On the morning of October
1st, I was lying on my bed, reading, when I began to notice that
everything was vibrating. I immediately thought a big truck must
be driving by. But the shaking got worse. I couldn't figure out what
was causing it. In all my 22 years, there's one thing I am sure of:
the ground doesn't move. Then, as the shaking continued, I realized where I was. This was Southern California. I was experiencing
something that before this I had only heard of, that was only a
theory. I was in an earthquake. Then I ran out-side, which I later
learned was the wrong thing to do. There was no place to go. I
watched the electrical cables sway between the telephone poles,
like a jump rope between two kids. It was a mind-altering experience. The one thing that I had assumed, up until then, could not be
shaken, was shaken. Sure, I knew about earth-quakes theoretically
but, until then, experience had taught me, deceptively, that the
ground doesn't move. It's stable. It's dependable.

What do you think can't be shaken? People are looking for
something stable, solid, unshakeable that they can found their

life on. In modern American culture that has been sold as "the relationship," romance. We even have a holiday, Valentine's Day, to celebrate what our culture believes is the pillar of life. It's an entirely unnecessary holiday since most couples already celebrate their anniversary but we feel that what we now call "the relationship" is so important that it deserves another holiday, even if it makes single people feel lonelier than ever. Novels — even a whole genre of novels ("the romance") — songs (from the seventies, "You Light Up My Life"), movies, all, unquestionably hold up the vision that "the love of my life" is the meaning of life. But like sitting on a balsam wood chair, we've put so much weight on that relationship we've crushed it. So now the culture that has made the most out of the romantic, marital relationship in the history of the world also probably has the highest rate of divorce in the history of the world. We're so known for being unfaithful to our marital commitment, Singapore's first Prime Minister, the late Lee Kuan Yew, warned Singaporean women that white men will divorce them quickly. (I was in Singapore at the time, 1990, to court my wife!) It is as if — I don't know for certain that this is the case but I suspect it — God saw the idol we were making out of romance and decreed to unleash a plague of broken relationships on us. Now "the relationship" (we call it) is shaken: judgment for making an idol out of something that was supposed to help us worship Him.

For traditional Chinese culture, the idol — often literally — is the family. Familism is the real religion of the Chinese, much more so than Buddhism or Taoism or Confucianism. The family is the one lasting, unshakeable institution, they think. The Chinese aren't the only ones who've made an idol out of the family; they've just been most consistent, taken it to a whole new level. In the movie Godfather 2, Michael senses a problem in his marriage and so asks his mother for advice. How is he to handle his responsibilities, as the "Godfather," without shaking the family, without losing his family? At first, his mother doesn't understand the question. She can't conceive that the family could be shaken. Michael has to clarify: "I meant, lose his family?" his mother, puzzled, speaking in Italian, insists, "But you can never lose your family." The

Chinese would agree. Not even death separates us from our family. We serve our family now, even our dead ancestors, by sending them food and money. China resisted the gospel because, some said, Christianity was an "ancestor-denying religion." The judgement for that, I think, is a communist government that disrupted families. During the "cultural revolution," from 1966 to 1976, the Chinese Communist Party taught a total dedication to the party at the expense of the family. Children were encouraged to inform on their parents, leading some of them to be executed. It taught people to betray the family. One song the Red Guards taught the children went, "Mother is close and father is close. But they won't be as close as chairman Mao." Family affection was considered one of the "old" habits that was to be replaced. Then, soon after the end of the cultural revolution, in 1979 China instituted a "one child policy" that limited the family, encouraged gender-selective abortions, resulting in, now, as many as 30 million young men who, statistically, won't be able to have families of their own because there are not enough women to start families with. The family has been shaken.

Many people think that the thing that can't be shaken is money. If you have enough of it, your life will never be too troubled; you can buy your way out of any problem. Some around us right now are working hard to get rich so that when they have enough to establish their life on, they'll be on "solid financial footing" (the term used by investment consultants) for their retirement, their old age, and then, maybe, they think, they can come back to church; they'll have time to work less and serve God more then, when they're stable. Of course, being rich didn't save Kobe Bryant (who had a net worth of $500 million — half a billion — and died, tragically with his daughter, at forty-one) or Steve Jobs (founder of Apple who died of cancer at fifty-six) or Ivan Semwanga, a Ugandan socialite, worth $8.8 million in Uganda and South Africa, who when he died of a heart attack at age thirty-nine, his friends at the funeral, instead of throwing handfuls of dirt into the grave, threw handfuls of cash. Money makes a poor substitute for earth. It is shaky ground.

What we think of as unshakeable, dependable, solid, is what we'll base our life on and we'll show that by living for it, above all, which is the definition of worship. Worship — "worth-ship" — is giving worth to something with your life, the priorities your life demonstrates, by the time, the interest, the passion, the energy, the money, the consideration that you're willing to pour into something. In Hebrews 12, we see worship, giving worth described in three words.

Grateful

First, worship is grateful. That means it is joyous, celebratory, glad that we have received something we didn't earn. There's a I-just-won-the-lottery aspect to worship, except that our winnings are not based on blind luck but on the love of a gracious Father. Hebrews 12:28 says we have received a gift, a kingdom — the good news of the rule of God in our lives. We haven't had to work or fight to bring it in. It was granted to us, by grace. Because it is God's Kingdom and it was donated to us by God, it can't be shaken. It doesn't depend on our will or effort. Since it's not based on luck or work or our flighty will, it's not shakable. That's worth being grateful for.

In that earthquake in Los Angeles, everything around me was shaking and there was no place to go to get away from it. If there had been a stable place to flee to, I would have run there as fast as I could. But there wasn't. Everything was quaking. That's the way this world is. All the things we are so sure are stable — every relationship, every nation, every religion, everything that has been made — can and will be shaken. Americans of the Great Depression generation and just after, know the economy can be shaken, that banks and business can go bust. But they don't think the government can be so they buy US savings bonds. Singaporeans of the same generations saw the Japanese oust the British, the British come back, inclusion in and then expulsion from Malaysia, independence foisted on them, with a teary Prime Minister admitting that they might not make it. They know that governments can be shaken too. But we have received a Kingdom that cannot be shaken. For that, we should be grateful. The writer says that through that gratitude we can then offer to God worship. Give him worth.

Because gratitude leads to worship, then worship is not merely a discipline that we subject ourselves to in order to gain points with God, like our exercise, a chore they must endure. If that's how you look at coming together with the church to worship, you would be better off staying home. If the singing and the sermon and the Lord's Supper is so dreary, then don't come. Of course, you would be much better off if you changed what you think is giving worth to, that the rule of God over your life, the singing and hearing the Word of God with his people that you once regarded as so much drudgery, that now it is one of the most important things to you; the highlight of the week. Even when we don't sing your favorite songs and the preacher is flat (as he is sometimes), still the sheer fact that you assembled with other of God's people and were reminded that God brought you into his Kingdom by grace, makes you grateful.

Some people won't cross the street to go to any church. Some will cross a dangerous ocean to be able to go to a biblical church. The Puritans crossed the Atlantic and founded New England for just that. Almost every Christian will say that worship is important to them. But few have proven it as boldly as did the Puritans who came to America to plant a "City Upon a Hill." John Allin, the earliest pastor of the church in Dedham, Massachusetts insisted that "only the hope of enjoying Christ in his ordinances" was enough for them "to forsake dearest relations, parents, brethren, sisters, Christian friends and acquaintances, overlook the dangers and difficulties of the vast seas, the thought whereof was a terror to many . . . and go into a wilderness, where we could forecast nothing but care [worries] and temptation." In other words, it was worth coming to America, even when the only thing they could be sure they would experience were problems, dangers, shortages; but it was worth it just so they could worship God biblically. They gave worth to God by forsaking dearest relations, facing the terrors of the ocean and the wilderness just so they could be in a biblical church.

Another leader of the second generation of Puritan New England, Samuel Wigglesworth, said, "A pure and undefiled religion was the great thing our ancestors had in their view when they cast their eye towards this wilderness for a habitation" (*An Essay for Reviving Religion*, 1733, p. 34.) Another leader from the same time, Increase Mather, wrote,

> It was in respect to some worldly accommodation that other Plantations were erected, but Religion and not the World was that which our fathers came hither for . . . Pure Worship and Ordinances without the mixture of human inventions was that which the first fathers of this colony designed in their coming hither. We are the children of the good old non-conformists. (*An Earnest Exhortation to the Inhabitants of New England*, 1676.)

That worship was important to them, they proved by braving a dangerous ocean on rickety sail boats. Because we now know that we've been given a Kingdom that can't be shaken, we worship, we give worth to God, to his Word, to his people. It's the natural response. Since we received this Kingdom, and since it is unmovable, let us offer to God worship.

Acceptable

Acceptable to who? In our consumer society where the customer is king, we think we need to please the people who give the offerings. Sing the songs and give the messages that they want to hear. But worship must be acceptable to God. That means that he is the One who approves of what we do in worship. This is the heart of what we mean by "God-centered" worship: it is done God's way. The Lord Jesus said, the kinds of worshippers the Father is seeking "must worship in spirit and truth" (John 4:24.) Don't overlook the key word "must." Hence the Puritans believed in what Reformed theology calls "the regulative principle of worship": the corporate worship of God is to follow the commands of scripture. Worship is not a favor we do for God which he is bound to accept, as long as we intend it to be worship. We must let God regulate what is worship. If we don't have that attitude, our worship isn't acceptable. There are so many people, even church people, who, when you ask them what are we supposed to do in worship will answer, "Whatever opens our heart to God." What they mean is, "whatever gives us a sense of joy and fulfillment." The principle that regulates worship for them, then, is themselves, their feelings, their sense of what they think is spiritual, what works in attracting people, the customer, like in any other business. They assume that they are the customer. But in the second commandment — you shall have no graven images — the Lord insists that worship be done his way. It didn't matter if the image wasn't another god, if it was supposed to be a symbolic representation of the Lord or an icon of some saint; it didn't matter that in their culture everyone used images in worship; that it made them feel religious. What mattered is what God said. It was God who regulated worship.

We see this illustrated brilliantly in Leviticus 10:1–3. There the sons of Aaron thought they could worship God in any way they thought best. They didn't abide by the Law; they didn't do things God's way. It wasn't acceptable worship. The principle for them was convenience, what they thought was common sense. They took any fire and tried to use it with their incense. They immediately learned what it says in Hebrews: "our God is a consuming fire." Fire from God came out and consumed Aaron's sons. The Lord spoke to Aaron, through Moses (no words of condolence): "Among those who approach me I will show myself holy; in the sight of all the people I will be honored." They thought they could take any fire they wanted to burn the incense on. They ignored what God's Word said about where the fire was to come from. They got "fired," so to speak. God is dangerous.

Reverential

Since God is dangerous, acceptable worship is "with reverence and awe." Reverence and awe are two sides of the same coin. Reverence is a holy fear. Hebrews 12:29 begins with "for" or "because." The Greek could literally read, "for indeed," emphasizing that this statement is the basis — the reason — for worshipping with reverence and awe: "for indeed our God is a consuming fire." This is like saying, "Be careful with that wire because — for indeed — it is high voltage." In Hebrews 12:29, it is "Revere God because, indeed, there is danger in approaching Him."

We sometimes become so used to speaking of God, reading his Word, handling his ordinances, such as the Lord's Supper, that we lose all fear of them. The Corinthians had apparently done that with the Lord's Supper. They took it anyway they pleased, each whenever they got around to it, with no thought of anyone else. The wealthy who arrived early would take it, perhaps take so much they got drunk off the wine. They wouldn't wait for the poor slave who had to work late to arrive. Maybe they wouldn't even leave any bread or wine for him. They didn't think about the Body. Paul says that that was the reason some of them were sick, and some even died. God afflicted them. This is why we prepare ourselves with our covenant and serious prayer before the Lord's Supper, that we'll not take it thoughtlessly; that we'll recognize that we're dealing with a dangerous God.

Evangelical worship is sometimes scorned as lacking reverence. At one service someone threw out a beach ball to be bounced off the fingertips of the assembled people. An observer was so put off, he drifted off into the Eastern Orthodox Church. I once went to a Baptist church where the Lord's Supper was served like an after thought, with a man picked out, impromptu to say a quick prayer before serving it to the people. It so lacked anything like reverence, it's the only time I've passed on receiving the Lord's Supper. Prayer, in many churches, is treated like a punctuation, a way to mark a transition in the service, a notice, like a traffic light, that the direction of the service is about to change, not really an address to a holy God. Prayers often feel slap-dash, completely unconsidered. If the President of the USA was visiting our church, we'd consider every facet of our reception, every word with which we addressed him. But the King of Kings comes and we give it no planning, at least little with him in mind. This is why some evangelicals feel drawn to lectionaries, liturgies, and set prayers passed down through tradition. I don't blame them too much but that's unnecessary. The Bible comes with a collection of songs and prayers in the middle and we have a model prayer to guide us, the Lord's Prayer. Preparing for every service, I write out a prayer based on the psalm we are to read and sing. We read, sing and then pray a psalm so that the psalter effectively serves as our lectionary. It's the best lectionary since it's inspired. Reverence for God's word means we infuse our worship with it.

Awe is more positive. Awe is an overwhelming feeling of wonder of facing something or someone so much greater than you; so much greater that you become aware that you lack the capacity to fully understand how much greater. You're humbled by what gives you awe. Like the sense you get when looking into a star filled night sky of how big God must be. People will travel hundreds or thousands of miles just to stare into the Grand Canyon to be filled with awe. One of the goals we should strive for in our church is a sense of awe about God.

Colossians 3:16

"Let the word of Christ dwell in you richly, teaching and admonishing one another in all wisdom, singing psalms and hymns and spiritual songs, with thankfulness in your hearts to God." Colossians 3:16 consists of one sentence with four parts: dwelling, teaching, singing, and thanking.

First, we are to "Let the word of Christ dwell in [us] richly." We "let" means we open ourselves up. We are allowing the Word to be active in us. We are making a decision that God's Word can have its way in our lives. We will change our thoughts and feelings according to what it says. It is the "Word of Christ," whether that be about Christ, even from the Old Testament, or about what Christ has done, the gospel. Let the gospel live in you richly. Let it be like a spoiled child that gets everything, all the attention, it wants. Let the gospel consume your attention and interests. That Word is to "dwell," to live continually, in us. It lives in us in a particular way: richly. It is to flourish in our hearts and minds.

That's why we are to strive for scripture saturated services. For our church, we read from the Psalms. We sing a psalm; we pray a psalm. We hope our other songs are scripturally based. We read our passage. I set it apart from my words — by saying "hear the Word of the Lord" and "may the Lord add his blessings" — because his Words are higher than my words. The sermon should be expository, taking its main point from the passage and frequently drawing our attention to the open Bible in front of us. Worship is about getting us to encounter and absorb the Word of God so that it is living richly in us.

Church, again, is not a building. It is the gathering of God's people around the Word of God. We can gather around the Word, and so have church, in a home, in a park, at school, in a gym, and if the Word of God is central then we've been the church. Or we can gather in a church building but, in reality, be gathering around other things: "the relationship," the family, money, a concert, a show, a personality, or whatever. What makes it a Christian church is if we gather around the Word of Christ. If we're giving worth to God, we'll cross the street, cross the county, cross state lines, even cross an angry ocean to get to worship.

Then, the second part: teaching. We are to "teach and admonish one another in all wisdom." Notice that this is not just addressed to the one "preacher." It's to you. You too should look for opportunities to teach and admonish one another; maybe before and after the service; make contacts and see each other during the week, e-mail or call or message or Facebook and teach and admonish one another or share with someone new during the week. We worship by giving God worth in talking to others about Him.

Psalm Singing

Then, the third part: singing. "Singing psalms and hymns and spiritual songs." Modern evangelical worship has impoverished itself by not singing psalms. They are a rich source of lyrics that often challenges the shallowness of our man-made songs. Singing psalms introduces into our singing themes modern hymnals and contemporary songs avoid, like judgment. Judgment is a common theme in the Bible but look at the subject index of an average hymnal for hymns about judgment. You may not even find the category. Psalms about God's judgment, however, are not rare. The book of Psalms is God's hymn book, placed in the very center of our Bibles. Psalms aren't just poetry to be read but lyrics to be sung. The psalms are inspired by God for the purpose of being reflected back to God. So it makes sense that we use them in our worship. Puritan churches sang psalms. The Reformed churches still have a heritage of psalms paraphrased for meter and rhyme which can be sung to the tune of familiar hymns. They make tremendous hymns in their own right. Our church sings through them all, one psalm per service, at least. We're commanded twice in the New Testament to sing them. Why would we not want to?

However, the New Testament doesn't command us to sing only psalms. "Hymns" and "spiritual songs" are not just other words for psalms. We know from 1 Corinthians 14, where Paul says some were "singing in the Spirit," that they weren't only singing psalms. We're also to let the Word of Christ dwell in us richly through "hymns" (songs of human composition, like the "Carmen Christi," the "song of Christ," in Philippians 2) and "spiritual songs."

Joyful, hopeful people sing. Singing has always had a part in Christian worship because worshipping Christians are joyous people, even if we're not always happy. Some psalms also teach us how to maturely be unhappy. We have laments because sometimes we need to know how to be unhappy. Joyful people know how to be unhappy.

Whether we're singing happily or lamenting, we give worth to God. We should not have the attitude that singing is just the warm up act for the preaching. It's what the people do to fill up a little time, get in the right attitude, set the mood, and the real substance of a church meeting is the preaching. Paul plainly puts singing as not something other than worship, not even as something separate from letting the Word of Christ dwell in you richly. It is a way of doing that. Our singing is one technique, one means, that we use to let the Word of Christ dwell in us richly.

In God-centered worship, the main goal is not to walk down memory lane or sing the newest, most up-beat song, to entertain ourselves or people from the world. It is to get us to have the Word of Christ dwell in us richly, so that we would worship the Lord acceptably, with reverence and awe. The whole debate between singing exclusively old hymns or contemporary music is nonsense to the Christian to whom worship is important. When the purpose is seen as letting the Word of Christ dwell in us richly, to worship acceptably, with reverence and awe, then we go in search of the music and songs that do that, new or old. The principle, then, is what music and songs helps us remember, sing, and dwell on the Word of Christ. Psalms are indispensable because they are inspired. Worship should be important enough to us that we will sing through the Psalms, learn some 500 year-old hymn or change to a new style if it will help us, as the church, worship, give worth to God.

Then the fourth part — thanking — takes us back to where we began with Hebrews 12:28: "with thankfulness in your hearts to God." The beginning and the end of our worship is the thankful attitude of our hearts that we have not gotten the bad things we deserve but we have been given the good things we don't deserve. Yes, we are dealing with a dangerous God — a consuming fire; a God who strikes people dead for offering just any kind of fire they want on the altar, for taking the Lord's Supper any way they please. But we can be thankful to him for his grace. We can be thankful that we who so easily overlook the truly important things — the God who is a consuming fire — and become so attached to all the things of this world, all the things that will be shaken, that he who cannot be shaken takes hold of us. We are set on a foundation that will never experience an earthquake.

How Much Worth Do You Give to Worship?

When, in 2018, I wrote an article (in *Themelios*) responding to Eastern Orthodox apologists, I learned that the kinds of people most drawn to convert to Eastern Orthodoxy are theologically educated evangelicals, people with masters degrees in theology, who take their faith seriously. They look at many evangelical churches and see how shallow, how flippant, how irreverential their worship is. Evangelical worship often has little awe of God. The worth is all on how God can help our relationship, our family, our bank account. God is so often used to serve whatever shakable thing our culture idolizes. Such people then look to the Eastern Orthodox church, to "smells and bells," and think, because of its ancient rituals, that this has stood the test of time and so is unshakeable. They buy the line that it is the early church. It isn't. The true early church strictly prohibited icons. Further, it has been shaken too, like marriage has in this country or the family in China. It's been shaken by Islam and communism. Almost every country that was Eastern Orthodox has fallen to Islam or the official atheism of communism. There is no substitute for having the "Word of Christ" richly dwelling in you.

Jesus himself was a worshipper. He gave worth to God with his whole life. Even though he dreaded the pain, despised the shame of having the sins of people placed on him and punished for them, still, for that, he gave thanks. On the night he was betrayed, he took up the bread and wine symbolizing his own body to be broken that very day and — incredibly — gave thanks to the Father for it. He had gratitude for it because in it he would satisfy the wrath of God against our sins, making it possible for the love of God to give us an unshakeable Kingdom. He gave thanks. How much did worship mean to Jesus? What was it worth? He crossed not just an ocean but heaven to take on flesh and then have that flesh broken for us so that we would worship God in Spirit and truth. For that, he was thankful.

CONCLUSION

The Idea of a Church

ON A TRAIN PLATFORM in Singapore I realized the need for the church's main diet to be expository preaching, for the Bible itself to be our lectionary, even if it doesn't come marked for which passage to read every Sunday. Teaching at a Bible college there, I had come to see the doctrines of grace from scripture. My first class was teaching on Romans and Galatians. When I got to Romans 9, I was faced with a decision: do I really believe the Bible or am I going to perform some interpretative gymnastics to make it fit my preconceived theology. Up until then, I described myself as "an Arminian with a high view of the sovereignty of God." When I saw Romans 9:16 — salvation doesn't depend on man's desire or effort but on God's mercy — I realized I had to change what I believed or stop claiming to believe the Bible. That night, I told my new wife, "Today I became a Calvinist." She said, "It makes a lot more sense, doesn't it?" "Yeah." It also dramatically effects how we worship and preach the gospel.

About a decade later, I was preaching at a church retreat in Malaysia that went surprisingly well. The pastor's wife said I should become a pastor. I had just completed my Ph.D. studying the New England Puritans. I decided that if I'm going to do that, I'm going to revive their spirit, if not always their practices, here summed up in seven pillars. I've been seeking to do that over the past two decades.

What's surprised me most seeking to plant a "neo-Puritan" church characterized by these seven pillars, in the small-town South, is not that being Reformed — teaching the doctrines of grace, God-centered worship, church discipline —would be resisted. I expected that. It's not that being intentionally inter-racial would be resisted, as I expected that. (Recently, calls for the church to attend to crossing ethnic lines have come to be reflexively condemned as "woke.") I'm a little surprised at how asking members to be active has led to some having problems and leaving so they can go be passive consumers in another religious theater. But what's surprised me the most, what's been the most resisted and most offensive to people, is the church itself; the idea of the church, of a body of believers knit together; a "church family." That idea is now foreign to our culture. But I thought, if it could be grasped, it would be attractive, desirable. You would want to be a part of the church once you got a glimpse of it.

Consumerism has eviscerated the church so that, as Mark Dever said, "churches in modern America have nearly vanished. The idea of the church . . . has dissolved in the acids of the reigning individualism of today's culture" ("Church: The Message of 1 Corinthians," Oct. 10, 1999.) The consumer, then, steps into the church looking for a spiritual product, like a shopper at a grocery store. Many churches' response to that is to encourage it. They encourage it by appealing to the very forces of consumerism that are breaking down their church. They market the church in order to get potential customers' business: the lighting, the band, the untucked shirt and jeans all carefully crafted to appeal to the "unchurched" consumer; there is a special series on child-rearing or whatever felt need appeals to the moms; the building feels like a mall and the speaker communicates like a friendly neighbor leaning over a fence giving lawn care advice. This, too, is not new.

Many traditional churches, the OTR, draw in consumers with a gospel sing or a revival or a "home-coming." Gimmicks to get customers in the door are commonplace, some now so long-established that they are considered sacred traditions. The "old time religion" is largely a figment of the consumeristic "second great awakening." Both old and new church marketing assumes that the "unchurched" — a term that smells more like consumerism than evangelism — are inviolable consumers. Overcoming that basic assumption about the church will hopefully be the product of establishing these seven pillars.

I wish I could guarantee that setting up these seven pillars would transform consumers into disciples. The problem is that we're dealing with people who have heard the word "church" over and over for their lifetimes, but they've never really seen the church. I'd quote Vince Lombardi before a team of pro-football players, holding a football, "Gentlemen, this is a football." (In other words, don't think you know what it is just because you've supposedly been around it your whole life.) But we swim in the acids of individualism and think it's just part of nature. When consumerism is so much at the core of who modern people are, they might conclude, "Sure, I like your doctrine and the people are nice but this other place has a slide running down the middle of the stairwell!" and proceed to choose their church like parents choose to go to Chuck-E-Cheese.

What's surprised me the most is how offensive some people find the idea of the church. Jonathan Leeman called it "the surprising offense of God's love." People may want to come to churches, to be informed about the Bible (to a point), to be inspired to be better people, to receive "insights for living," to expose their kids to positive messages, to be entertained by heart-felt music. They may want to go to a church. They just don't want to be a part of the church. That's because in this culture, the idea of the church is radically counter-cultural. We live in a culture that screams, if it doesn't make you happy, right now, then ditch it — or him or her — and go find one that does, whether that be a restaurant, a satellite TV service, or a spouse, or a church. It's all disposable and consumable.

There's no way to change that but by doing the hard work of nurturing healthy, Biblical, counter-cultural churches. We do that by erecting these seven pillars and praying that on them a new culture comes alive, a new body breathing in the fresh air of God's Spirit. We've seen some great examples of members being the church. We've seen fruit. When I broke my leg, about three months before finishing this book, and had to have emergency surgery, two ladies from our church came to visit my wife. I had baptized one about a decade earlier. The other we had led out of the Jehovah's Witnesses. When my wife told me that they had come, I lay in the hospital bed that night and thought, "That's the church."

We may not be big but, for now, by God's grace, we're healthy. I wish I could boast in large numbers. But I'd rather have a small, faithful church family of contributing members than a large organization of consumers coming for the show. Thankfully, by God's mercy, Covenant Reformed Baptist Church has survived and continues to spread the Word of God. Maybe under a more gifted, mature pastor, it would have grown more. Maybe these pillars, erected by more skilled workmen elsewhere will transform more consumers into worshipers and revolutionize the church. May it be.

Author

John B. Carpenter is pastor of Covenant Reformed Baptist Church (Danville, Virginia, www.covenantcaswell). The messages of this book were presented as sermons which can be heard at the Covenant Caswell YouTube channel. You can connect with him through Twitter, at JohnCarpenter64.

He has a Ph.D. (Lutheran School of Theology at Chicago), studying New England Puritanism, a Th.M. in Systematic Theology (Trinity Evangelical Divinity School), a Master of Divinity (Fuller Theological Seminary), and B.A. from Samford University for which he was an athlete.

He is married to Mary Yeo, of Singapore, and they have two sons.

He is the author of

- "The Beginning of Days: A Response to Jeremy Lyon's "Genesis 1:1–3 and the Literary Boundary of Day One," *Journal of Biblical and Theological Studies*, 6.1, 2021, pp. 153–168.

- "Genesis's Definition of Israel and the Presuppositional Error of Supersessionism," *Trinity Journal*, 42 NS, 2021.

- "The Early Church on the Aniconic Spectrum," *The Westminster Theological Journal*, 83, May 2021.

- "The 1620 Project: Puritanism and the Ideological Founding of America," *Touchstone Magazine*, May/June, 2021.

- "A New Definition of Puritanism, A Cross-Disciplinary Approach," *The Evangelical Journal*, Vol. 36, 1, Spring 2019.

- "A secular Jew makes a surprising discovery about Christians and American slavery," *Acton Commentary*, April 17, 2019.

- "Rise of the Social Justice Contras," *The Christian Post*, March 12, 2019.

- "Answering Eastern Orthodox Apologists Regarding Icons," *Themelios*, December 2018.

- "The Social Justice Statement and the Scandal of the Evangelical Conscience," *The Christian Post*, October 6, 2018.

- "Recovering From Strange and Friendly Fire", *The Christian Post*, November 5, 2013

- "New England's Puritan Century," *Fides et Historia*, 2003

- "Genuine Pentecostal Traditioning," *Asian Journal of Pentecostal Studies* 6:2 (July 2003).

- "New England Puritans: The Grandparents of Modern Protestant Missions," *Missiology*, Vol. XXX, No. 4, October 2002.

- "The Fourth Great Awakening or Apostasy?" *Journal of the Evangelical Theological Society*, December 2001.

- "How Firm a Foundation: The Puritan Roots of American Liberty," Acton Institute, 2001.

- "Puritan Missions and Globalization," *Fides et Historia*, 1999.